a CARPENTER'S LIFE
as told by houses

a
CARPENTER'S LIFE

as told by houses

LARRY HAUN

The Taunton Press

The Taunton Press
Inspiration for hands-on living®

The Taunton Press, Inc.
63 South Main Street
Newtown, CT 06470-2344
e-mail: tp@taunton.com

Editor: Peter Chapman
Copy Editor: Seth Reichgott
Jacket and interior design: Carol Singer
Layout: Lynne Phillips

The following names/manufacturers appearing in *A Carpenter's Life as Told by Houses*
are trademarks: Aermotor®, Chevrolet®, Dempster®, Estwing®, Greyhound®,
HardiPlank®, iPod®, Lego®, Levi's®, Masonite®, Monopoly®, Nike®, Paslode®,
Playstation®, Plexiglas®, Plumb®, Romex®, Sears® and Roebuck, Singer®, Skilsaw®,
Speed Square®, Styrofoam®, Trus Joists®, U-Haul®, Viagra®, Walmart®, Wincharger®,
Wonder® Bread, Xbox®

Library of Congress Cataloging-in-Publication Data

Haun, Larry.
  A carpenter's life as told by houses / Larry Haun.
      p. cm.
  ISBN 978-1-60085-402-6 (hardback)
  1. Dwellings--United States--History. 2. Vernacular architecture--United States--
History. 3. Housing--United States--History. I. Title.
  TH4809.U6H38 2011
  694--dc23
                          2011021612

Printed in the United States of America
10 9 8 7 6 5 4 3

To all who care for our planet. Don't give up.

ACKNOWLEDGMENTS

With love, I thank the many friends and relatives who took time to look for and send me old photos from their collections.

This book is being published because of two people at The Taunton Press:

Justin Fink, a senior editor at *Fine Homebuilding* magazine, who encouraged me to write my story.

Peter Chapman, an executive editor in the books department, who convinced the good folk at Taunton to publish this book. It has been a joy to work with him.

TABLE OF CONTENTS

THE FIRST TIME I SAW LARRY HAUN swing a hammer, I knew
that I wasn't nearly as good a carpenter as I had thought.
It was 1987, and I had only recently walked off of a job site and into
a job at *Fine Homebuilding* magazine. The Taunton Press was starting
to make how-to videos, and one day the video producer invited me to
watch an instructional tape from the United Brotherhood of Carpenters. The star was a tall, thin man in his 50s.
Over and over, he drove sixteen-penny spikes with two licks—one to
set and one to sink. The nails disappeared so fast I wondered if some
magician's trick were secretly pulling them into the wood ahead of the
hammer blows. I never saw Joe DiMaggio play baseball, but those who
did describe his movements as seamless and fluid, as having no beginning and no end. One observer quipped, "He made the rest of them
look like plumbers." That's how I felt watching Larry Haun drive nails.
Not long after I saw that video, Larry wrote his first article for
Fine Homebuilding. He went on to write countless more, along with several books, mostly about the production framing techniques he helped
pioneer on the frenzied tract developments of southern California.
His amazing skills were due, at least in part, to the fact that he kept at
it long after most carpenters move on to jobs that are easier on
their bodies.
It's telling that when Larry finally did retire and stopped building
houses for a living, he joined Habitat for Humanity and started building them for free. I would like to have been there the first time Larry
Haun showed up on a Habitat project. At the peak of his powers, Larry
and his two brothers could frame an entire house in a day. I imagine
the Habitat foreman asking Larry if he had any experience and him
replying, "Some."
On the surface of it then, this book is the story of Larry's life as
seen through the houses he has known, lived in, and built. This

experience ranges from the sod houses of the Great Plains (his mother grew up in one), to the kit houses sold in the Sears catalog, to the little boxes of the post–World War II housing boom, to the McMansions of today. And given that we now take plywood, nail guns, and the overflowing shelves at The Home Depot for granted, it is fascinating to read about a time when carpenters made their own framing hammers and soaked nails in paraffin so they'd be easier to drive. But it would be a mistake to think of this book simply as a carpenter's memoir or as a history of houses.

As prodigious as Larry's carpentry skills are, and as fascinating as the span of his career has been, neither is what makes him remarkable or this book so worthy. Larry is indeed a great carpenter, but he is hardly typical. Despite a lifetime spent on raucous job sites brimming with testosterone, Larry is a quiet, unpretentious man who has long been more interested in Buddha than Budweiser.

Larry didn't write this book to impress anybody. He's looking for deeper truths. When he reflects on the houses in his life, it is not so much to marvel at how far we've come, but to see what we've lost, and most important, to see what we can learn. For him, it is a small step from *where* we live to *how* we live. Gently and humbly, he raises questions about the decisions we've made as a society, about how we treat each other, and how we treat this planet that we live on.

In this entire volume, otherwise filled with charming tales and timeless wisdom, only one assertion rings false. Having grown up on the high plains of western Nebraska, in an uninsulated farmhouse with no central heating, Larry says he was always cold, even in the summer. He claims that cold has dogged him to this day, which leads him to conclude that all his efforts, all his struggles, the reason for his existence, has been to do whatever was necessary to keep himself warm. Hardly. Anyone who has ever known Larry will attest, and readers of this book will soon discover, the reason for his existence has been to warm others with his remarkable spirit.

Kevin Ireton
New Milford, Connecticut
July 2011

MY MOTHER TOLD ME that I started to take a real interest
in the few carpentry tools we had around home when I was seven
years old, back in 1938. She said I would sit on the sunny side of
the house for hours taking apart orange crates that came to our
village once a year. For a boy with nothing but homemade toys,
these sweet-smelling soft pine wooden crates were the mother lode.
Our curved-claw hammer was missing a claw, so I pulled the
small nails out of the crate with a pair of pliers. Once the crate
was apart, I fashioned the wood into play objects, a small house,
a wagon, boxes, and shelves to hold things. It was here that I
learned one of my first carpentry lessons: to hold my thumb a good
distance from the head of the nail. Bam-ouch-blood!

Our nearest hardware store was 30 miles away, so when something broke, we fixed it. Tools became as much a part of my life as
food. I can now be grateful for those days because they allowed me
to learn a trade where I can create with my hands. By the time I was
19, I was a union journeyman carpenter in Los Angeles, where the
sun shone most every day. Making decent wages, I was able to study

at universities for 13 or 14 years, not to collect degrees, but to satisfy my curiosity. Besides building houses, I taught night school at a community college for nearly 20 years—carpentry to apprentices, Spanish to people who just wanted to talk to their neighbors, and even deaf children (and their parents), helping them integrate into mainstream schools. I was able to travel, buy and remodel a simple house, raise a beautiful family, and in my later years become a writer trying to help others be master carpenters.

Some of my travels took me to countries where I saw firsthand how many thousands of people live on the edge in tin and cardboard shacks. I recall an early morning walk along the Pasig River where my wife, Mila, lived in the Philippines. Near her home many families are crowded together in unstable houses that hang out over this once pristine river, now the recipient of all human waste. A teenage girl with clean, colorful clothes and an armful of school books emerged through a small opening from her tin "house," which measured no more than 8 ft. by 12 ft. I was encouraged by her bright eyes and smile. I peeked inside and spotted a colorful cloth covering a wall and a flower in a vase. For her, this simple house was a place where she could dream her dreams.

At the other end of the spectrum, as a contractor, I was once invited into a palatial home near Los Angeles to discuss a remodeling project. A servant seated me in a reception room full of thick carpets, fine furniture, and museum art. Maybe ten minutes later a couple entered and we began. It wasn't long before I felt a chill move through me, not from the temperature of the room but from the evident hostility between the man and the woman. Let's just say that I passed on the job.

I can't help but wonder about the relationship between people and their homes. How do these vastly different dwelling places affect the people who live there? How have I been shaped by the houses I've lived in? Who and what would I be if I'd been born in an upscale mansion or a shack by the river? *A Carpenter's Life* is my way of looking at these wonderings.

To state the obvious, we can't choose our place of birth. Given a chance, I would not have chosen to have been born in 1931 in a refrigerator called a balloon-framed wood house out on the treeless high plains, the short-grass prairie, of western Nebraska in the middle of the Great Depression.

I have lots of good memories from those times, but being cold is not one of them. In the 18 years I lived there it seemed to me that I was always cold, due mainly to the constant wind that blew down across the snow-covered sagebrush hills out of Canada and into my life. There was never a question about whether the wind was blowing or not. Rather it was about how hard and how cold it blew. Turn your back on our iron kitchen stove and you could see your breath. Whatever the temperature was outside, that was the temperature in our bedrooms, even when Mother warmed the sheets with her flat iron. We did have those summer days when I would play on the lee side of the house, but the chill never left. I could never get warm all the way through. (In retrospect, I sometimes feel that all my efforts, all my struggles, the reason for my existence, has been to do whatever was necessary to keep myself warm.)

The house had no insulation, no electricity, no running water, no indoor plumbing, and no central heating. Flannel sheets, down comforters, wool socks, and thermal underwear were something I knew nothing about. Even now, far from snow and wind, as I sit here in Oregon, I can still feel that chill in my feet. Long, lean,  and hungry-looking I am, with not much natural insulation on these bones, growing older daily. By the time my blood is pumped from my heart down through my long body to my toes, it has cooled considerable. Take my guard down for a minute and there will be icicles on my nose.

These days I take time to teach a granddaughter, Julia, and a grandson, Jonathan, how to hammer nails, cut wood to size, and build things we need around our homes. They won't follow my path, but they will know how to fix things as they grow into adults. If they stay here on the Pacific coast, most days they can work without wearing a jacket. And me, I'm sitting here with my feet propped up near a wood fire that keeps the icicles at bay. 🦋

"We did not think of the great open plains, the beautiful rolling hills, and winding streams with tangled growth as 'wild.' Only to the white man was nature a 'wilderness' and only to him was the land 'infested' with 'wild' animals and 'savage' people. To us it was tame. Earth was beautiful and we were surrounded with the blessings of the Great Mystery."

—Luther Standing Bear, SIOUX CHIEF

CHAPTER ONE

The Soddy

NOT EVERYONE lives in a wood-frame house warmed by a central heating system with double-glazed windows, HardiPlank® siding, and solar panels for electricity. There are other ways to build our homes. Nipa huts, for example, are ideal for the Pacific islanders who live near the equator. Made of bamboo with a thatched roof, these huts allow breezes to pass through and ease life lived in heat that can be oppressive.

Tepee structures fashioned from long poles and covered with hides made it possible for the Native peoples of our Great Plains to take their homes with them as they followed the migrating buffalo. Mongolians also have a mobile home. The yurt has a lattice structure made of wood pieces brought from the lowlands. The traditional felt cover comes from sheep wool. A yurt can be taken apart and carried on the backs of yaks as these nomadic people follow their herds to different feeding grounds.

The Q'ero people live in the high Andes Mountains far above the timberline. They build from local materials—rocks and grass.

The Q'ero people live in the high Andean mountains of Peru far above the timberline. There are no trees at 13,000 ft. These descendents of the Incas build their homes out of rocks. Farther south, in the lowlands of Chile, the Mapuche live in rukas, round buildings made from the wood that's plentiful in their part of the world. Many people in El Salvador still live in their traditional earth-pole homes.

This is the way it has been throughout our long history. People need a place to live and love, a shelter where they can eat, sleep, and carry on their family activities. The Navajo with their hogans, the Inuit with their igloos, the Bedouins with their tents, and the Ndebele people with their colorfully painted homes in South Africa all built from materials at hand.

Their buzzwords were not "build locally" and "build sustainably," but that is what they were doing. They couldn't bring in lumber from Oregon, siding from Australia, drywall from China, and tile from Italy. The materials they were using—earth, snow, bamboo, and grass—came back year after year. They were green builders of the first order.

AND SO IT WAS with the birth house of my mother, Elizabeth Brennan. She was born in 1897 in a one-room sod house. It was located not far from the North Platte River ("too thin to plow, too thick to drink") near a small town named Lisco in western Nebraska. Just a wide spot in the road until it was incorporated in 1909, Lisco was named after Rube Lisco, an early cattle rancher in the area and employer of my grandfather. Not far down river is Chimney Rock, that landmark sandstone spire that let pioneers on the long trail to California and Oregon know where they were.

Chimney Rock, a sandstone spire, greeted immigrants traveling along the North Platte River in western Nebraska in the 1800s.

It's important to recall that this vast inland sea of grassland was the traditional home of the Lakota and Northern Cheyenne peoples. Can any of us feel how painful and frightening it must have been for those who had lived on these plains for hundreds of years to suddenly be seen as trespassers? One day they rode freely in search of good water, good hunting, and a place to camp and care for their children. The next day the prairie was being invaded by settlers who were putting up houses and fences saying this land is mine! Native people knew that they belonged to the land. They saw the land as the source of life, not profit. How could the land belong to them or someone else?

It has always seemed strange to me to think that a plot of this earth we live on could actually be owned by anyone. It's a bit like owning air. But really, can a piece of this isolated planet that exists in a galaxy of 100 billion stars be owned by me? Maybe one day someone will figure a way to charge us for the air we breathe. The earth has been in existence for 4 billion years, plus or minus, or so I am told. We as a people have been around for 250,000 years, maybe more. So who owns whom?

Earth has given us clear notice that it doesn't need us, but that it will allow us to be renters here as long as we behave ourselves. If we misbehave, we will receive an eviction notice and forfeit our cleaning deposit. As temporary residents, we have left quite a mess in our wake: foul air; toxic waste dumps; denuded, clear-cut mountains; dirt-clogged salmon streams; and melting ice caps, not to mention poverty and hunger. A pretty impressive list that may not make our landlord happy!

The Homestead Act, passed by Congress in 1862, opened up huge, virgin tracts of Native land to immigrants hungry for a place to live and put down roots. If you were 21 or over, you could settle on 160 acres, live there for five years, and be granted full ownership. This was the reason for a huge migration of people in our country. By 1900, 600,000 homestead claims had been filed. Staking a claim meant that every settler had to build some type of home on "their" land and survive through some difficult times before they became the owner. The majority of these settlers "starved out" and didn't make it beyond two years before moving on. An uncle told me that there would come a day when some just gave up, either from hunger, discouragement, or loneliness. When that day came, they hitched up a team to a wagon, loaded a few possessions, and left everything else behind—house, chickens, hogs, and horses—and went back home or headed farther west.

The early takers were from all walks of life: businessmen, farmers, tradespeople, and women with their children. All were hungry for land and a new life. They had first choice of the rich, flat, bottom lands along the Platte and other rivers that are abundant in eastern Nebraska. They found ideal farmland there, great for raising their signature crop: corn. There were some trees in eastern Nebraska for log house construction, especially along the waterways. The later folks, like my mother's parents who arrived in 1891, had to push on hundreds of miles farther north and west to the rolling hills of the western part of the state, covered by the prairie grasses on the high plains. They made the long trip out of Missouri

My relatives as they prepared to head west with their children and few possessions to settle on free homestead land on the short grass prairie in western Nebraska.

"As the saying goes, there were miles and miles of nothing but miles and miles."

with their children, a few possessions, and lots of dreams, all hauled by team and wagon. Once there in western Nebraska, they staked out their claim, unloaded their farming tools, cooking utensils, a few clothes, and bedding, and readied themselves for hard work and tough times.

Even today, when you drive through those western grasslands, you will notice the scarcity of trees. Many people called it the Great American Desert. My grandmother said that there was not one tree in sight either on the prairie or along the river. As the saying goes, there were miles and miles of nothing but miles and miles. It's hard to be a tree-hugger in that part of the world. It was easy, especially at night, to become disoriented and lost without these landmarks to guide you home.

We have forgotten what it means to be out in the dark of night. Most of us live in the city, where night has been turned into day. Even in the country, we are never far from an electric lightbulb. But stand in the middle of the Great Plains far from a farmhouse on a moonless, starless night and try to see your hand in front of your face. "It's as dark as a stack of black cats" was a common saying. On those nights, the only directions you can know for sure are up and down.

So without trees, these early settlers had few poles or sawn wood to work with. The only building material readily available was the earth lying underneath their feet. *Pachamama* as they say in Peru—Mother Earth. This high plains earth was solidly held together by the roots of hardy, winter-tested grasses like little bluestem, Indian grass, and buffalo grass (named after the millions of bison that had been grazing this land for thousands of years).

The first settlers to arrive after the Homestead Act used shovels to cut out sections of earth, called sod. Gathering sod strips along with planting fields and gardens, caring for themselves, their

Sod strips were cut from the prairie, loaded on a wagon, and brought to the building site.

children, and their farm animals was hard work to say the least. Finally, in the 1880s, the breaking plow with a curved steel cutting blade, called the "sod-buster," became more common. This plow laid long strips of sod, 12 in. wide and 4 in. thick, over flat. My mother's father harnessed a breaking plow to his team of workhorses and cut pieces for his own sod house. Technology came to the rescue.

Sometimes I hear that technology will get us out of the earth-warming, poverty-ridden, overpopulated mess we find across our small planet. What is it that makes me doubt that statement? Maybe it is my feeling that the changes we need today will come not from the head, but from the heart. I sometimes think of what Lily Tomlin once said: "Things will most likely get worse before they get worse." That seems to be the trend.

The earthen sod strips, called "Nebraska marble" by some, were cut into lengths about 3 ft. long, measured out by a notch on the handle of a shovel or ax. Each strip weighed about 50 lb. The strips were loaded onto a wagon and hauled by a team of horses or oxen to the chosen building site. People tried to pick a site that was on the lee side of a hill, if that was available, to offer some protection from the winter winds. The actual building size was laid out by "stepping off" the dimensions. Ten full steps on one side measured around 30 ft. Corners were marked with stakes, and the diagonal was stepped off to square the building.

Once the sod strips arrived at the site, they were laid grass side down, two strips wide to make a thick wall, a solid barrier to the cold wind and winter snow. The second course started with half a sod strip to lock the courses together. Special attention was given to the corners, making sure the sod strips interlocked. Every three or four courses, a row of sod was laid in the opposite direction to tie the two layers together and to stabilize the walls, which were built up to around 6 ft. or so on the low side and 7 ft. on the high side. Walls of different heights created a shed roof with a pitch or slope that allowed water to drain.

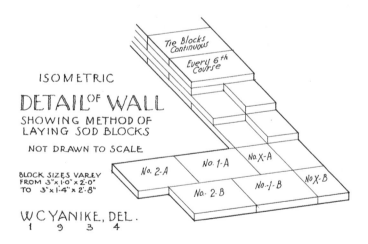

Laying up sod strips for a soddy is a little like putting together Lego® blocks. The strips are laid in double rows, for insulation and stability.

A one-room soddy left little space for privacy.

Holes were left for a single door, often to the south, and two or three small windows to the east and west. Windows were the most expensive part of a "soddy" and were often hard to come by. No openings were put in the north side for further protection from the icy winds that blew across those treeless plains. The sides of the layered sod were smoothed and evened out with a shovel. Any crack that could let in the wind was filled with mud. At times, after the sod had settled for a year or so, the walls were plastered with a mixture of water, clay, and ashes from the stove. Kalsomine, or whitewash, made of lime, chalk, and water all mixed together, could be used to brighten up the interior.

My mother reckoned that their one-room house was around 16 ft. by 30 ft. These, of course, were the outside dimensions. With walls 2 ft. thick, inside dimensions were closer to 12 ft. by 26 ft.—312 sq. ft. of living, sleeping, eating, and cooking space. This is about the size of a living room by today's standards. Some privacy was offered by closing off sections with a quilt or other cloth hanging from a rope stretched from wall to wall and attached

"People could only dream about a wood floor. They lived on floors made from compacted earth that was periodically wet down with water to keep them hard and dust free."

to the ceiling-roof. My mother's family consisted of her parents, five brothers, a sister, and herself. These were crowded quarters for nine people, especially as baths and underarm deodorants were hard to come by.

The door and windows were held in the openings by wooden pegs driven into the sod through holes drilled in the frames. Actual doors were often nothing more than a piece of canvas secured over the opening. A space of 4 in. or 5 in. was left at the top of the frames to allow for the sod to settle without breaking the glass. These spaces were filled with rags or grass to keep out the wind and snow. People could only dream about a wood floor. They lived on floors made from compacted earth that was periodically wet down with water to keep them hard and dust free. At least you didn't have to mop the floor if you spilt a cup of coffee. Wooden floors were added in time when the settlers made enough money to buy the materials.

At times, I wonder where our obsession for super-clean houses and super-clean bodies comes from. Is it that "cleanliness is next to godliness"? Is it because advertisers are constantly urging us to buy more of their soap and clean up our act? All of our recent ancestors, maybe not by choice but by the fact that they lived next to the earth, often had well-earned body odors and lived in dwellings that were not easy to keep clean.

Lumber for door and window headers, rafters, and roof sheathing was not readily available before the completion of the transcontinental railroad in 1869. When they had lumber, headers were a 2×8 laid flat, roofs were built with a 2×6 ridge and rafters and sheathed with 1×12 stock. Before 1869, people who had a few dollars made the long round trip to the Black Hills in South Dakota with a team of horses pulling a wagon; there, they picked up sawn wood or poles from the lodgepole pine tree. These lightweight trees grow straight and tall (which made them easy to transport by Native people, who used them in their tepees).

Our building materials were paid for by slowly collecting the profits gained from selling chicken eggs and shipping cream from my family's milk cows to a dairy in eastern Nebraska. These dollars were taken from money that had been carefully stashed away in a quart mason jar. (There were no bankers around in those days receiving huge bonuses.)

Trade in the early days was mainly on a barter system, as few people had ready cash to pay for services. People exchanged help when building homes, preparing and harvesting fields, working with livestock, and having babies. Real money was scarce. The coming of the transcontinental railroad built along the Platte River helped, allowing people to ship their cans of cream and crates of eggs to larger population centers in the East. The first

large building to process cream into butter and cheese opened in Fremont, Nebraska, near Omaha, in the early 1880s. Many a settler survived to stay another year because he or she had some chickens, a cow or two, and a cream separator.

The cream separator, a pioneer family's treasure, was used to separate cream from milk. These ingenious devices were still in common use when I was working on farms and ranches in the 1940s. Raw milk was poured into the top container. A crank was then turned, forcing the heavy milk to the outside and leaving

The hand-operated cream separator was a valued possession for early immigrants. They were able to sell cream from their milk cows for real money.

the lighter cream in the center. Spigots were opened, allowing the skim milk to go into one container and the rich, thick cream into another. Some cream was saved for hand-churned butter. Part of the skim milk was used for cooking and drinking. The rest was fed as slop to the hogs.

Once the walls of the soddy were up it was ready for a roof. Early settlers had to make do with what was at hand. They often made a roof framework from willows growing near the river or from branches of cottonwood trees farther to the east. If tar paper was available, a layer was put down on the roof structure before being covered with a grass thatch and then with strips of sod laid down with the grass side up. Without tar paper, which was often the case, rainwater soaked right on through. The sod made for a living roof that blossomed with wildflowers in the spring—sunflowers, goldenrod, larkspur, sweet peas, and Indian paint-brush were among the many. Roof sod was cut 2 in. thick to lessen the weight. Eventually, the settlers who stayed on could afford shingles or corrugated tin for their roofs. The problem they faced then was to keep these materials in place. The constant wind that often blew with savage ferocity would carry their roofing materials into the next county.

It was primitive living for sure, but in many ways, sod houses were ideal for the plains. Inside, they were actually warm and cozy in the winter and cool on hot summer days. It is difficult to explain how long and bitter the winters were. If you have never experienced a wind-driven blizzard of snow howling across the plains with tem-peratures way below freezing for days and even weeks at a time, what can I write to make you feel chilled to the bone? Carelessness in those extreme conditions often meant being caught outside and freezing to death.

Even as a teenager in the 1940s, I recall hearing tales of the blizzard of "88" from old-timers. It was often called the "children's blizzard," because it came on a school day in March, trapping many students in their schoolrooms. Those that ventured out, trying to get home, were soon disoriented by whiteout conditions. Some bodies were not found until the spring thaw. Families were often so devastated by the loss of their children that they gave up and moved elsewhere.

> "The constant wind that often blew with savage ferocity would carry their roofing materials into the next county."

The soddies were fireproof. (Fires used to roar across the prairie in the fall.) Dry grass, a lightning strike, and a gale wind coming down out of Wyoming were all it took to burn thousands of acres. An old Texas cowboy, Dan Jordan, once told me that the fires often traveled faster than a horse could run at a full gallop. Many of his stories were what people called tall tales, but this one rang true.

Once the house was in livable condition, a water well along with a cellar had to be dug and other structures built. Until the residents had a well, water often had to be hauled from the river or a distant spring by team and wagon. Fortunately, wells could sometimes be dug by hand with a shovel, as the water table near the river was only from 6 ft. to 25 ft. down. Deeper-dug wells existed, but the danger increased the farther down you got. Water was absolutely essential, so people were willing to take the chance. They had to work in a confined place with little or no light, filling a bucket with earth that could be hauled by rope to the surface. Risky business because the sides could cave in, especially in sandy soil, and take the life of the person down in the hole. It was next to impossible to extract a buried man, so blessings were said and the hole became their grave. May they rest in peace. I recall hearing a story about one of my mother's brothers, who was buried up to his neck down in a well. Rescuers were able to get him out alive, but fear kept him on terra firma from that day on.

Cellars were dug close by the house with a shovel and, like the house, covered over with a structure that would support a thick layer of sod. These underground storehouses were necessary for survival. They were used to store potatoes, carrots, turnips, and other root crops for winter use. Settlers had to raise and then dry or preserve most all the food they would eat during the winter. Items like green beans, tomatoes, corn, garden relish, and even chickens were cut up, cleaned, and preserved in mason jars. Cabbage was sliced or grated, placed in 5-gal. or 10-gal. crocks, covered, and left to ferment into sauerkraut. Eggs too were placed in crocks filled with salt brine, ready for use when the chickens rested from their laying duties. The same was done with pickles and beets preserved in dill-vinegar brine. In good years, prairie fruit like chokecherries, sand cherries, wild plums, currants, and buffalo berries could be made into jams and jellies or dried in the sun and eaten like raisins. All were carefully stored in the cellar to keep them from freezing during the winter months.

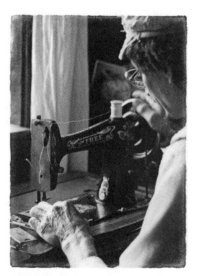

Now and then, my mother's family had fresh meat from a butchered cow, pig, or prairie animal like an antelope. This was often shared with neighbors, because no one had refrigeration for storage. When money was available, they could buy supplies of cornmeal, wheat flour, sugar, and salt at the markets in the small towns that sprung up along the railroad. Sourdough

Preparing to mend clothes for my children on my grandmother's treadle-operated sewing machine.

bread and cornmeal mush were staples. They didn't have the option of sending their children over to the supermarket to bring home processed food, and fast-food places were still way in the future.

One of the first necessities, of course, was to build an outhouse. Then came a chicken house, followed by a stable for the horses and harnesses. An amenity my mother spoke of was a lean-to attached to the southern, sunny side of the main house. This was used as a kitchen in the summer months. A sod wall was put up on the windward side, and the rest of the structure was built from poles and covered with grass thatch. When the weather allowed, the family cooked and ate outside, free from the crowded conditions they lived in for most of the year, welcoming the fresh air and summer smells. Women would take out their ever-present sewing machines for the good light needed to sew and patch worn clothing.

These amazing, treadle-operated sewing machines were highly valued by immigrants. The machine my grandmother had was a "Free," which is very similar to the more common Singer®. Everyone knew how to sew. Her Free machine is the one my mother taught me how to use when I was seven. I in turn taught my children how to use it, and now it is with my daughter, Risa, who is passing on sewing knowledge to her children, teaching them the fundamentals of making and patching clothes. We have had to replace the round, leather belt that goes from treadle to machine several times. Other than that, it seems like the machine will last forever, unlike many of the "throw-away" items on the market today.

I ASKED MY MOTHER one day before she died what it was like to live in a soddy. She said they had to get used to living in close quarters. Her main dislike was that they could never control the bedbugs and fleas that hid between the sod layers and came out at night to feed on them, leaving itchy welts on their bodies. Her mother would give the children a chicken feather or a willow stick dipped in kerosene, which did little to dislodge these critters from their hiding places between the strips of prairie earth. Rodents too liked to burrow into the sod and look for scraps of food in the dark. Mother said it was not uncommon to feel little feet scampering across the bed covers at night.

Sleeping space was limited. Mattresses—little more than cloth bags stuffed with grass—had to be piled in a corner during the day. Boys slept in one bed and girls in another. At least other bodies helped keep you warm.

Because of the small windows, the interior light was always poor. With only two kerosene lamps, my mother's family lived and worked inside in half darkness even on a sunny day. They could only dream about picture windows and skylights or an electric bulb that would bring light to a dark room.

It doesn't rain much in western Nebraska. The average precipitation, including snow, runs around 18 in. a year or so—not a lot, unless you have a roof that leaks. Every time it rained or the days warmed enough to melt the snow on the roof, my mother's job was to rescue their sleeping mats, bedding, pillows, and clothes and move everything to a dry spot. In those days, there were no plastic tarps available to cover everything. Rain would wash the dirt out of the roof sod and drip mud on everything on the inside. Storms in the western part of the state can arise suddenly and come at you with a fury that is awesome and fearful. Wind-driven rain meant that the sod walls could be damaged and in need of repair.

My mother did not like snakes. There are snakes aplenty in the Upper Plains, the most numerous being rattlers and bull snakes.

Now and then a bull snake would find its way through the roof and drop down into the living area. She passed her dislike, especially of venomous rattlers, on to me and my siblings. I know now that these snakes do more good than harm by keeping rodents under control. But once your mother teaches you differently from an early age, gut reaction overcomes intellectual knowledge. I tolerate snakes, but I don't like them. Once, a nephew asked if I wanted to hold one of his "pet" snakes. I declined.

The most difficult part about living in a soddy, my mother told me, was the isolation and constant work faced by immigrant women. They often lived far from neighbors and other women with whom they could share their lives. And their lives were not easy, often filled with an aching loneliness.

Both parents had to work. "Root hog or die" was the way they put it. There were no 8-hour work days; rather, it was from "can see to can't see." Women especially had a heavy workload. They not only were responsible for all the work inside the house, but there was agriculture work as well: planting a garden, milking cows, feeding calves, and caring for chickens. Then consider the effort it took for a wife and mother to make and mend clothing for her family, see that they had food daily, and were somewhat clean. Picture a one-room house with seven children, no electricity or running water, and only an outside, two-hole toilet. Disposable diapers were unheard of in those days. Night waste stored in a bucket was carried out each morning, even in the dead of winter, when temperatures could drop well below zero.

Water for bathing had to be pumped by hand and hauled in from a well. Once inside, it was heated on a stove that burned willow branches, twists of grass, sunflower stalks, or dried cow chips (manure) picked up off the prairie. Washing clothes was a monumental task, which involved scrubbing items on a washboard. I have seen the knuckles of my mothers' hands raw and bleeding at times. Blessed be the automatic washing machine, for it helped free women from drudgery!

Hanging clothes out to dry was no picnic either. In winter, the cold, dry weather would take much of the moisture from wet clothes hung on the line and chill your fingers to the bone. Frozen stiff, pants, shirts, dresses, and all were brought back inside and placed around the room like so many statues to finish the drying process.

If you look at old photos from this time and place, you will often see a birdcage hanging outside the soddy. Many women kept a bright yellow canary in a cage for its precious, uplifting song. This brought a little beauty into their lives and helped them maintain their sanity. It is not hard to understand how some settlers

The children who went to school in a soddy often had a man for a teacher in pioneer days.

succumbed to this harsh, isolated, and often lonely life and literally went insane or took their own lives. Mental illness was not a known affliction in those days. I recall hearing stories of people who went mad and had to be shipped off to the east to an "insane asylum" in Hastings. Those that made it through were definitely strong men and women! Those that survived the best had a sense of humor, allowing them to laugh when many of us would have cried. My mother was one of those strong women, gentle yet firm, who could see the humor in events.

She went to school in a soddy. Unlike most women in those days, she was able to attend classes at a normal college in central Nebraska (Kearney) and became a teacher. She went on to teach in a school made from straw bales in the nearby vast, almost roadless, grass-covered Sandhills. In 1920, she moved farther north to Harrisburg, Nebraska, to teach in a wood-frame school. It was there that she met my father, and there that I was born.

THE SOD HOUSES played an important part in rural Nebraska. Most are gone now, but I recall seeing them around the town of Harrisburg during the 1930s when I was a child. In 1946, when I was 15 years old, I worked all summer in the far northwest corner of Nebraska for a rancher. I remember it well because the water there was strongly alkaline, which made me go to the bathroom much more often than normal. The rancher's original homestead was a soddy that had been added on to with frame structures as the family grew. The soddy itself was used as the kitchen—cool in the hot summer and warm in the cold winter, with the good smell of homemade bread drifting out the open door. When I think back to my time as a hard-working, hungry teenager, that smell is ingrained deep in my system and marks those times as good.

So when I hear people longing for "the good old days," what are they saying? Are they remembering the smell of fresh-baked bread? No one I know wants to return to those hardscrabble days where their very survival was threatened on an almost daily basis. Even at best, life was tenuous. Most immigrants didn't make it and had to move on or are resting in forgotten graves covered once again by prairie sod.

I think what we miss, what we long for, especially if we take time to listen to our hearts, is to reconnect with the earth. Our ancestors trusted the earth. Even if they woke up fearful in the middle of the night, they knew the earth was still there, supporting them, giving them life. Yes, the work was hard, but after a day you could see what you had accomplished: a field plowed, grain harvested, bread made, eggs collected, a cow milked, a garden planted. You knew it was the earth that gave you this food that allowed you and your children to live.

Our longing, our restlessness comes because for the last 100 years or so we have been crowded into huge, sprawling, often smog-choked cities. In some of these cities you can literally walk miles and never see an open piece of ground. We are stuck in these concrete jungles because that's where the work is and because there is no longer any "West" calling us to move on. Our ancestors were hunters and gathers for 250,000 years or more, living on a prairie either here or there. A few generations have given us tremendous technological advances—TVs, iPods®, cell phones, frozen dinners, and processed food. What hasn't changed is our earth-based DNA passed down to us by a thousand generations of mothers and fathers who came before us.

We miss touching the land, the smell of turned-over sod, the coming of springtime, and seeing the bounty and beauty of wildflowers. Deep inside we remember the smell of the air in the total stillness as the storm approaches from the west, a stillness that allows us to listen to the low, growling rumble of thunder heralded by strikes of awesome lightning. And then, after the storm, we are greeted by the startling brilliance of a double rainbow stretching across the western sky.

We want to once again speak the names of the wildflowers and the grasses and to know where the meadowlark hides its nest. We long to pick and taste the wild currants, plums, grapes, and choke-cherries that grew along the watercourses. We yearn to see the sudden, pale blush of the prairie rose that blooms for a day or two and is gone. We miss the sight of the Milky Way, that river of stars overhead that once seemed to be part of everyone's life. We want to slow down and have time to be with and cherish our loved ones. We long to feel, sometimes in the evening, that gentle breeze that comes, touches our faces, and tells us who we are. 🌿

"If you have heard it, you know it is a sacred thing . . . If you have not heard it, you had better hurry to where they still sing."

—Mary Oliver, "LEAD"
(writing about the song of the loon)

CHAPTER TWO

The Straw Bale

STRAW BALE HOUSE construction is undergoing a revival in this country. There seem to be many reasons for this. First, the basic building material, dry straw left over from harvesting grains like wheat, rye, and rice, is easily obtained at a reasonable cost from local sources in our farming states. Much of the work needed to build with straw bales can be done by semiskilled workers. Community-minded people, friends, and neighbors can come together for a "bale-raising" party.

As citizens become more conscious of how their activities affect our world, they want to use products that are friendlier to our environment. "Environmentalist" is no longer a four-letter word among growing numbers of people. Things and people do change. (Remember not so long ago, when it was cool to smoke cigarettes?)

Straw is a natural material that is nontoxic and biodegradable. You can actually live in a straw bale house without fear of breathing in and getting sick from the toxic fumes emitted by many common construction products. Who wants to breathe polyvinyl chloride (used to make carpet backing) or formaldehyde fumes that come from material used in making cabinets, plywood, or sheets of strand board? The energy used to cut and bale straw is less than it takes to make wood or steel products. Further, a bale house is well insulated, so it needs less energy to keep it warm or cool. One final reason for the resurgence of interest in straw bale construction is this: People who build with straw realize that this medium can allow them to be creative. Straw can be sculpted into forms and shapes that make a house into a warm and inviting home.

My mother, Elizabeth Brennan, wearing 1917 clothes bought with a few dollars saved from her teaching job.

MY MOTHER, THE SCHOOL TEACHER, taught school in a bale house when she was a young woman in 1916 in the Sandhill country of western Nebraska. These country schoolhouses were built by the thousands all across the farm states as people strove to make sure their children received a basic education in readin', 'ritin', and 'rithmetic. In that they were quite successful, as the literacy rate among these isolated homesteaders was high.

First day of school, Joe, Larry, Loretta, Margaret and Jim

My brothers, sisters, and I (second from left) lined up for a "first day of school" photo in 1936.

Men seldom went beyond the sixth grade, but at least they could do their numbers, read the local newspaper, and sign their checks when they had money in the bank. It was a badge of honor to be able to sign your real name and not an "X" that had to be witnessed by someone else. These men may not have had much formal education, but they were no strangers to hard physical labor. Imagine the effort it took to prepare a livable, survivable place on their homestead for their families and livestock with not much more than what was available locally.

My mother was contracted by the school board to teach all eight grades. The pay, she said, was $40 per month plus room and board with a ranch family almost two miles from the school. With this money she was able to buy a piano for her own mother along with a camera and a few clothes for herself. When her mother died in 1936, she had the piano transported 100 miles or so to our house in Harrisburg.

The piano was shipped to Kimball by railroad (the Union Pacific) and then the final 30 miles to our small village by horse and wagon—quite out of tune by the time it arrived, I'm sure. But everyone needs some music in their lives, no? The camera, a box type with leather bellows that Mother kept pliable with a little sewing machine oil, was another lifelong treasure. She prized the camera because it allowed her to record a few events in her own children's lives. She always took a picture of us children at the beginning of a new school year, all lined up, standing in birth order, fairly clean, and ready to go.

Unlike in other areas of our country, there were few trees on the plains where the European immigrants built their soddies. There were even fewer trees in the adjacent Sandhills. Fewer, as in none. Sod houses were out of the question because the grass roots couldn't hold the sandy soil together as the prairie earth did elsewhere. With the advent of a usable horse-powered hay press in the late 1800s, immigrants found a way to build their homes with the only material available: prairie grasses.

Once early settlers had the horse-powered hay press, they could use local grasses pressed into bales to build their houses on the treeless plains.

For thousands of years, people had been cutting grasses and grains with a scythe, threshing out the seeds for food, and then piling the rest in stacks to use throughout the winter. Once people had access to framing lumber for building barns, they began to store hay in the barn loft, making it readily available to feed stock animals in the space below during the winter. The problem was that loose hay quickly filled the loft space. The hay press compacted loose grasses and straw into bales that were tied together by hand with twine or wire. These rectangular bales, averaging around 36 in. long and weighing about 50 lb., could then be stored in the loft space. The fact that they could be stacked to make walls would seem to be an obvious next step. The first straw bale house in Nebraska was built in 1896 or 1897.

> **"The first straw bale house in Nebraska was built in 1896 or 1897."**

Putting up hay stacks with a team of horses in the Sandhills before the hay baler became common.

A FRIEND TOLD ME recently that he *had to* travel the length of Nebraska on Interstate 80, 435 miles from Wyoming to Missouri. The emphasis was on had to, as the trip for him was unredeemable. He consumed inordinate amounts of coffee to keep him somewhat awake as he drove straight-arrow down this unending road bounded by nothing but endless fields of corn, millet, soybeans, and other boring crops! Well, what could I say? There is "a road less traveled."

I would have suggested he take Highway 2 through the center of the state and into the magical land of the Sandhill country. If we are hurrying just to get from one place to the next, we will always miss the magic present in these rolling sand hills: the sky, sun, flowers, bugs, even the birds and the bees. Magic can only happen if we are willing to ditch our cell phones, turn off the TV, slow down a little, and leave a gap in our rattle-on minds.

The Sandhills of Nebraska, some over 300 ft. tall, were formed around 15,000 years ago after the last glacial age. Some say these rounded hills were formed from wind-blown sand, others from a glacial outflow, or maybe even by a giant tsunami coming down from the north. Whatever the source of this vast tract, it is there, all 20,000 square miles of it. These sensuous hills of sand cover about one-fourth of Nebraska and support both short and tall grass prairie. Elsewhere this prairie is mainly gone, but at one time it spread over many millions of acres on the Great Plains that exist in the center of our country. I have heard old-timers tell stories about riding through grasses that came up to the heads of their horses—the big bluestem, Indian grass, needles and thread, and wild rye that can withstand subzero winters and hot, dry summers.

The Native people knew this area well because it was home to a major food source: huge herds of bison. Early European settlers long considered it to be an irreclaimable desert full of wild animals and savage people and seldom ventured within its borders for fear

Women worked alongside men in the fields, especially at haying time. This woman standing tall is Helen Wilson, with her daughter Arlene, ready to do the work that needed to be done.

of getting lost. They had reason to be fearful. Even today there are few landmarks, roads, or people living there to help orient you back to what we call civilization, where we often live in crowded cities and spend endless hours on car-clogged freeways. I recall reading a statement from Gandhi when asked about our civilized world. His reply: "That would be a good idea!" It seems fair to ask: Would a civilized people do to their home place what we are doing?

It is hardly surprising that the Sandhills is the birthplace of the straw bale house. Where else in our country can you find such abundant grass without any access to lumber from trees? Midwestern people are rightly famous for being able to "make do" with what they have.

The Kinkaid Act was passed in 1904, only a little more than 100 years ago. This act allowed homesteaders to claim 640 Sandhill acres, one square mile of grassy dunes. Today this area is a productive cattle-ranching area supporting over 500,000 grass-fed beef cattle. Two of my mother's brothers, Earl and John, had ranches there that are still operated by their offspring.

The elevation above sea level of these soft hills varies from some 1,800 ft. in the eastern part to 3,600 ft. in the west. Over millennia past, these dunes have shifted position as the prevailing winds have moved the sand and blocked waterways, leaving the area without a natural drainage system. Rainwater stays mainly where it falls, forming thousands of lakes big and small feeding the massive Ogalala aquifer that lies not far below. It's the largest and most complex wetland ecosystem in our country. Believe it or not, Nebraska is not just one big cornfield.

With all the wetlands, it's no surprise that this area is a stopover place for many migratory birds. The king of these birds, in my opinion, is the Sandhill crane, a tall, grayish bird with a red beret. The

For centuries, thousands upon thousands of Sandhill cranes have been returning to the Sandhill country to rest before continuing their long yearly migration.

cranes come this way each spring and again in the fall. Often more than one-half million birds pass through in a season. They have been resting in this area for eons. They spend their days gleaning corn, other grains, and seeds from harvested fields and prairie grasses, resting and refueling for the next leg of their journey.

If you haven't heard or seen them, stop what you are doing. You can easily hear them out in the Sandhills because there is no freeway roar or city noise to dampen their call. Their distinctive mating dance is beautiful and etched deep in my memory. When they begin to arrive, thousands of them circling like a whirling tornado, from the far north or south, depending on the season, you can hear them coming all the way from the distant Wyoming or Kansas border. Even when they come in small groups you can hear their cooing, rattling call as they settle down to rest in Sandhill ponds and lakes.

This makes for a birder's paradise, where over the course of a year you can see more than 200 species: the greater prairie chicken, sharp-tailed grouse, soaring hawks looking for a meal, geese, ducks, and various sparrows. You may even get to see a whooper. Not many years ago, these amazing cranes were nearly extinct. Over the years, with abundant help from all of us, they have been growing slowly in number, from 16 birds in 1953 to several hundred today. They stand out in a crowd, the tallest bird in our country, some with an 8-ft. wingspan. They are whiter and even more majestic than their Sandhill cousins. My mother told of their whooping call early in the morning as they were mating. Mating can be something to whoop about, so they got that right.

How is it that most of us seem to be unmoved by extinction after extinction of different plants, birds, and animals in our world? Native Americans have a philosophy that speaks to me. They tell us not to do anything until we consider how it might affect the livelihood of the next seven generations. Everything on this earth is interrelated. All life is precious. All species are sacred in the sense that they are whole and enrich our lives. Do we enrich their lives or are we their enemy? Without them we are surely less than what we are. The loss of any bird, animal, or plant leaves a hole in our spirits and sadness in our hearts. We truly have lost a brother or a sister when any living thing becomes extinct, provable only to those with an open heart.

THE SANDHILL HOUSES were actually made from hay, not straw. Straw is the stalk part left over after harvesting the seeds from plants like wheat or rye. Straw is preferred over hay because it is dryer. The seeds have been removed so it is not as appetizing for rodents and cows. Huffing or puffing won't bring down a straw bale house, but watch out for a bunch of cows munching on your home.

On the first day of school my mother said that her students, all six of them from three different families, came, like her, by foot or on horseback. She had walked from her home and arrived early to start a fire in the iron stove and prepare for the day. She was, after all, not only the teacher, but also the janitor, nurse, disciplinarian, and caretaker.

Mother said that when she would first open the door to the school in the early morning, a moldy smell permeated the room. Students, girls in dresses and boys in jeans or overalls, well-worn and patched, took their seats on roughsawn benches and sat at their desks. Her teaching aids were flashcards used to help students learn the alphabet and basic math, along with a few books for them to read. During the winter months sometimes a rodent that was living in the walls would feel the interior heat and burrow to the inside. This was always a cause for the children to laugh. They didn't have iPods for entertainment. They had to settle for finding fun in rats poking their heads through the wall.

My mother with her students in front of their straw bale schoolhouse in 1917. It has been stuccoed with a clay-lime mixture.

Straw bale houses were relatively easy to build for the early immigrants. The construction is similar to laying up sod or bricks without mortar. The footprint of a house was laid out in a square or rectangle, and the first course of bales was placed directly on the ground around the perimeter, oriented toward the life-giving sun. Sometimes the house size was modified a bit so that a full-size bale didn't have to be shortened. The second course was started with a bale overlapping the first at the corner. When they came to the end of the course, a bale was cut and retied to fill the shorter space. The third course started again with a full bale overlapping the second row at the corner. This pattern was continued until the desired wall height was reached.

Probably the most difficult part in straw bale construction is lifting and placing the bales in place. The bales the immigrants used were around 50 lb., quite unlike the tightly packed bales of today that can weigh as much as 130 lb.

My mother was a lifetime walker, most often stepping out on the prairie in the early morning before anyone else was around. She was no "couch potato" who exercised because she was told to (come to think of it, there really were no couch potatoes back then). Walking was something she did daily until almost the time she died at 85 of "natural causes." She would tell us of her encounters as the sun began to spread its light into her life. Badgers, prairie dogs, deer, coyotes, and even skunks used to check her out.

She was quite wary of skunks. One of her brothers was once sprayed by an irritated skunk. They had to burn his clothes, wash him down several times with lye soap, and keep him out of the house for a couple of weeks before he regained his normal smell.

Mother did say that her walks back and forth to her school were quite pleasant, except in the winter when it was cold and snowy and the air was laced with a bitter wind. At times when the weather was really bad her host family would take her to and from school on their only saddle horse. One morning they were hit by a blinding snowstorm before they could reach the school. Such storms can arise without much warning in that part of the world. She said that they were almost instantly lost. Fortunately, many animals have a homing instinct. They gave the horse free rein, lowered their heads into the wind, and let him take them back home.

The door and window frames for straw bale houses were typically made from 3×6 lumber. These were cut to size, nailed together, and placed within the walls. For the door, the top piece was cut long to fit on top of the side pieces. Made in this way, it could easily support the weight of the roof structure. The door was usually placed facing the southern sun. Windows, small ones, were set into the wall on top of the second or third course. The 6-in.-

wide frames were set to the outside of the bales, leaving wide window sills on the inside. Bales were then cut to fit snugly against the frames. As with the soddy, there were seldom any openings on the north, the cold and windy side.

The majority of these pioneer buildings were never meant to be permanent, so few are still around. Much of their impermanence was due to the fact that the bales were placed directly on the ground and left unprotected from wind and rain. At times, after the bales had settled for a few months, a coat of plaster was applied both inside and out to protect them from moisture, cows, and rats. By far the main enemy of this building material even today is water that can eventually create serious rot and decay. Without a foundation, water will wick upward into the walls, making for a moldy-smelling home.

Speaking of water, few schools had a well, so school families kept students supplied by bringing cream cans full of water and

This straw bale church was built in 1928 and still serves the community in the small village of Arthur, Nebraska.

leaving them in the schoolhouse. Cream cans were ever present in ranch-farm areas. They were used to send valuable cream separated from raw milk to the east by rail to be made into butter and cheese. These cans came in various sizes, but the one most people had held 10 gal. Mother had to set the can on the schoolhouse stove in the winter because the water always froze solid.

Plaster was not a cure-all for deteriorating walls and moldy smells, but it did help. It was made from materials at hand, though Sandhill folk had to travel some distance to find clay to mix with straw along with lime when it was available. Before plastering, holes or gaps in the bales were filled with a mixture of clay and straw. I have been told that the first coat of plaster was watery and was swept on with a broom. Once this was dry, a second coat was applied with a trowel.

We sometimes forget how convenient it is to have an indoor toilet. This luxury was not available to most people living outside cities until after World War II, which ended in 1945. Old photos of country schoolhouses typically show three buildings: the actual schoolhouse and two toilets set alongside, one for girls and another for boys. It didn't take long to do your business in these toilets, especially when the temperature fell below zero degrees. No sitting in there reading *Life* magazine or *The Saturday Evening Post*.

Almost all of the Sandhill homes built from bales were load bearing, which means that the roof was supported directly by the walls. This way of building is known as Nebraska style. It is still possible to build straw bale houses like this, especially if you use super-compressed bales that can bear a heavier load. But because of state code restrictions, many straw bale houses today start with a timber or metal frame structure. These frames are built on a concrete foundation, which raises the bales above ground level. Posts are then placed along the walls to support the overhead beams that will carry the roof. Once the frame is in place, bales

There were thousands of country schoolhouses throughout the plains states, simple buildings that were close to the hearts of the early immigrants.

are placed between or around the posts, filling in the open spaces. This type of construction uses more lumber or metal but allows for larger window openings.

One of the mistakes made by many immigrants who lived in straw bale houses was not building a roof with a large overhang. This would have protected the bales from water that came off the gable roof, which sloped to both sides. It would have been possible to do this because dimensional lumber was more readily available by the time straw bale houses were being built in Nebraska. The bales were prepared for roof rafters by placing a 2×6 top plate on the outside of the walls. The plates were wired securely to long willow stakes that had been driven down through the bales about every 24 in. to help keep them stable against the force of gale winds. Willows were cut from plants growing along the streams and rivers. Rafters were often made from 2×6s and nailed to the plates.

The roof was sheathed with 1×12s and then covered with tar paper and shingles. Once all was in place, the gable ends were filled with cut bales along with hay stuffed in here and there to fill the gaps.

I doubt that the people at the time realized this style of construction—building with local materials—would become increasingly popular a hundred years or so later. The immigrants must have known that bale homes were much easier to heat than uninsulated, wood-frame houses. Holes where the bales came together had to be stuffed full with loose hay to stop cold air from filtering in and the windows were not double glazed. Still, the insulating factor of bales far outweighs that of a frame house with zero insulation that housed many a family in ranching country.

People have begun to realize that we need to try and build from materials at hand. Build locally, as they say. Increasingly, expensive wood products have to be transported long distances to a building site. Straw is a renewable resource. Mother Earth, treated with respect, faithfully gives us a new crop year after year (estimated to be 200 million tons per year by the U.S. Department of Energy).

People who live in these houses have told me they love the warm feeling generated by the wide walls. They say it is like being seated in your mother's lap with her arms around you when you were little. If you happen to be stuck living alongside a noisy freeway, rest assured that the inside of your home will be quiet. And once stuccoed and plastered, straw bale houses surprisingly offer better resistance to fire than most houses.

I HELPED BUILD a small straw bale bunkhouse in 1947 when I was a teenager working on a ranch-farm. We built it just like my ancestors did, except that we covered it with a shed roof that sloped in only one direction. Otherwise, the main difference was that this structure had a rough wood floor rather than a dirt one.

This is where I slept cool in the summer and warm as winter approached before high school began in the fall. I returned to the area 40 years later and looked for my summer bedroom. All that remained was a slight mound where the straw bale bunkhouse used to be—along with my memories.

My mother often told me about the Sandhill flowers she came to know on her walks back and forth to the school. Among the prairie grasses (sometimes you have to look closely because the grass is tall) you will find the prairie coneflower, primrose, milkweed, mallow, poppies, and even black-eyed Susans. How can life be hard when we have these joys to brighten our day?

Bear in mind also that the presence of milkweed and other flowers means that you will see the monarch butterfly as it passes through on its 3,000-mile journey back and forth between Canada and Mexico. We sometimes gripe about having to walk a few blocks to the store. The monarch makes this unbelievable journey, on schedule year after year, supported only by small, rainbow-colored wings. What kind of marvelous magic is that? It is for this kind of wonder that the overused word "awesome" can be said out loud.

Mother said that at times on her trip home she would lie quietly on a hillside smelling the fragrance of the wild mallow. She would watch the butterflies; the birds—greater prairie chickens, sharp-tailed grouse, hawks, geese, ducks, and sparrows; and the small animals—squirrels, jackrabbits, foxes, badgers, weasels—all going about their lives, as she lay there until the sun went down, catching that last "green glow" as the light passed below the horizon in air that was still free from pollution. Can this be called a waste of her time? 🦋

"Tell me how can a poor man stand
such times and live?"

—Blind Alfred Reed, 1929

CHAPTER THREE

The Old Frame House

BEHIND WHERE MY WIFE AND I live near the beautiful Oregon coast, there is a new house—some call it a starter castle—that has five fireplaces and seven bathrooms. One of our granddaughters says it looks bigger than her middle school. I understand it has adequate rooms and sufficient space for the couple and their dog when they come here now and then. Increasingly, we live in a society that builds big houses and fills them with more and more. Does this leave us, our children, and our earth with less and less? Is this sustainable? Is this what life is about? Please let me know.

I was born at home in a wood-frame house with less than 1,000 sq. ft. of floor space in the small town of Harrisburg, Nebraska (pop. 85). As Barbara Kingsolver says, it was right close "to the center of the middle of nowhere." The nearest doctor was 30 miles away, so a midwife caught me as I came into life from my mother. She was happy to see me and hold me in her arms.

"The town was populated by many more chickens than people."

The town was populated by many more chickens than people. My mother told me she was happy I was born in May rather than icy December. May is the time when the meadowlarks perch on the fence posts and sing their beautiful courting song. This was her signal that the long, often bitter winter was finally coming to an end. Blessed are the meadowlarks, for they bring sunshine!

My parents bought this house in 1930 for $900 with money borrowed from the Kimball County Bank. Built in the 1890s, the house came with about 4 acres of land and several small, deteriorating outbuildings. There were few trees on the property or in the town, other than the Russian Olive, which some say is more of a weed than a tree. What was most valuable was that the house came with a good water well powered by a Dempster® windmill. The water below this town was not an easily tapped reservoir. Rather, it flowed in underground streams that even a water witcher, or "dowser," could not always locate.

This was about the time my father, Henry, was elected to be county clerk. He was one of the few people in the entire county who had a college degree, and he was more than honest and worthy enough to be a public servant. But he was elected for only one term: Our voting neighbors found out that he was a Catholic and that was that. Religious tolerance was, and still is, rather elusive in some quarters.

Dempster and Aermotor® water-pumping mills sprouted like sunflowers all across the Great Plains. They were easy to repair and required only a steady flow of what was most abundant—wind. Now and then you had to crawl up the wooden tower to grease the

Windmills sprouted like sunflowers across the Great Plains. Powered by the ever-present wind, they provided early settlers with a constant source of good water for themselves and their animals.

running gears. And from time to time you had to pull up the well pipes to replace the leathers in the pump at the bottom of the well. Here was a truly green product that has mainly been replaced by electric pumps. I miss seeing windmills standing tall and straight with their fanned wheels turning, pumping water, and well rods creaking as they drew up this gift from below. Directions were once given by the location of a windmill: "Drive down this road a long ways until you see the windmill off to the right. Turn there, go through the gate, and drive a couple of miles on the dirt road. Their house is right over a small hill. You can't miss it!"

House water for drinking, cooking, and bathing was drawn up by pumping a metal handle attached to a cast-iron pump. I was told early on not to grab this handle in the winter unless I was

Children were given the chore of using a hand pump to bring up water for drinking and cooking.

wearing gloves. A warm, moist hand would instantly stick to a freezing handle, and skin could be left on the pump handle if you pulled away. If you ever froze yourself to the pump handle, I was taught to pour water over the hand. The water would release the skin cold, but unharmed. I had to free myself from the handle just once—it's the kind of thing that turns you into a fast learner.

HOUSE FRAMING changed little from the time of our terrible "un" Civil War until after World War II. Our house did have a concrete foundation of sorts, badly weathered and crumbling because the mix didn't have enough actual cement to hold it all together. Beneath the house was the ever-present cellar. It was a creepy sort of place for me as a small child, full of spiders, dark, and rather scary. This cellar, little more than a hole dug in the ground under the house, is where Mother kept row after valuable row of jars full of veggies, along with pickled beets and cucumbers from her garden, and chickens from our yard. This was our food for the wintertime. On the south side of the house there was a door to this cellar where we children used to sit and play, trying to soak up a bit of heat from the sun.

The actual construction of this house was much like one of the first houses I helped frame in 1950 in Los Angeles (see Chapter 9). A 2×6 sill was placed directly on the foundation to support the 2×6 floor joists. No foundation bolts were used to hold it securely in place. Our floor was bouncy because the floor joists were undersize for the distance they spanned. This was true also of the 2×4 ceiling joists, which caused the plastered ceiling to sag like a sway-backed horse. We really don't build them like we used to!

A favorite place for us children to play was on the cellar door located on the sunny south side of the house out of the wind.

Lumber for house building was not readily available, even though there actually were a few trees not far from where we lived in the hills to the south. They were mainly juniper and small pines, nothing large enough to be used commercially. Lumber had to be cut, milled, and shipped in from the Colorado Rockies or from the Black Hills in South Dakota. It was during this time that I came to love the pine wood being used in construction. When I was 8 years old, carpenters remodeled the local high school. I stood there and watched as they cut and fitted wood with sharp handsaws and chisels. Most memorable were the long curls of pine rising from a door as a worker moved his jointer plane down the edge. One carpenter made a particular impression on me. Even as a child, I knew he had much to teach me by the way he held and moved his plane. This tool was not really separate from his arm. They were one.

But it was more than just the wood curls. The smell that came from the wood was also just there. That sweet smell of pine is still lodged deep in my senses. It is even deeper than that. How to say this so it sounds believable? When I become mindfully quiet, I can actually feel the scent of pine in my heart and body.

THE JOISTS IN OUR HOME were nailed in place 16 in. on center with machine-made, rectangular-shaped cut nails using a 16-oz. curved-claw hammer like the one I had as a child. The floor was then sheathed with 1×12 pine boards that I could see when looking up from down in the cellar. These boards were placed diagonally across the floor to help strengthen the frame. All the wood members had to be cut by handsaw. Sheathing diagonally means that both ends of every board had to be cut at a 45-degree angle to fit on the joists, which meant lots of sawing for apprentice carpenters. Once the house was framed and finished, the floor was covered with straight-grained, tongue-and-groove 1×4 Douglas fir boards. Most likely this beautiful flooring material had made the long journey to western Nebraska from the Oregon coast.

I had an old 8-point (8 teeth per in.) Diston handsaw at home that was as dull as a hoe. I often wished for a three-cornered file—the type used to sharpen the saw teeth. My family, and the entire county, was "dirt poor," as the saying went in those Great Depression days. About all anyone owned was "the dirt on their body and the hair on their head," so no file was available. This is the saw that I used to make childhood toys. The material I had was mainly from wooden crates used to ship the bright-colored, sweet-tasting oranges that came at Christmas time. What a treat that was! The crates were made from a southern pine. It was a beautiful wood, fairly soft and easy to work—as long as your tools were sharp. I didn't have money to buy nails for my small projects. I used nails from the crates and also those I found looking through the ashes of an old barn that had burned down not far from where we lived. The nails had lost their temper in the fire so were not easy to drive without bending.

I also had access to the city dump, where people threw their castoffs. Most everything was being recycled, but now and then I would find a treasure I could use, like a thrown-away alarm clock. I would tinker with the clocks and often get them running again. I feel sad that our landfills are now largely off limits. Our culture has learned that everything is disposable, so landfills are full of precious resources, goldmines in my view. Will the day come when prospectors once again pick up their shovels and start digging in?

The hammer I used to nail together my projects was missing one of the claws. It was made from forged iron and was brittle. Someone must have broken a claw while trying to pull a nail from a piece of wood. It was quite unlike the straight-claw hammer I use today. I remembered it fondly in a 1996 poem (see the next page):

Childhood Hammer

A forged, cast-iron, 16 oz., broken-claw model, it was.
Three days younger than the hills to the south.
Twenty-fifth cousin to the fine chromed steel framer I use today.

Boxes to guard childhood treasures, bugs, snake skins, and butterfly wings.
Crafted together from clear, white pine orange crates.
Nails sought and found around a burnt-down barn.

Bent nails like stooped carpenters left drooping in the wind.
No way to draw either upright.
Both turning to rust and dust.

Damn, damn, damn, damn.
Finger split like the wooden handle dripping blood and pitch.
Coloring the pine boxes like a chicken-poxed child.

Forged hammer stayed behind.
Teacher of yet another generation of nail-pounders.
Leaving me to stoop, droop, and turn to rust and dust.

My elementary school was a two-room schoolhouse with one teacher per room. By the time I was in second grade, I had listened to and knew all that was being taught to those in grades 3 and 4. The only course I never mastered was cursive writing, taught from a blue book titled "The Palmer Method." One time our teacher asked us to write a poem. I handed in what I now know was a page of free verse. She gave me a lousy grade, saying that poem sentences had to rhyme at the end. I do remember, with fondness, the songs we were taught from the Methodist hymnal. No separation between church and state in our small world. I used to enjoy the "Winding of the Maypole" each spring when we danced around a pole, wrapping it with crepe-paper ribbons. Some say this was an old pagan rite to welcome spring.

Once the floor sheathing was down and nailed to the joists, the walls were built one stick at a time. The wall-framing method was called balloon framing. This means that the wall studs did not go to a bottom plate set on the floor like we do now in platform framing. The bottoms of the studs were nailed down on the sill plate, one stud alongside each floor joist. No production framing here. A top plate was marked for stud location at 16 in. on center. Window and door locations were also marked. Window headers were most often 2×4s laid flat, which worked fine unless the opening was large. The roof load, especially when weighed down with wet snow, caused a long header to sag in the middle. Next came corner studs that were nailed in place one at each corner. They were braced plumb (straight up and down), and a string was pulled across the post tops.

On the first house I helped to build in Los Angeles, my job was to go along like the old-timers did. At every stud location, I set a piece of 2×4 on the bottom plate, and then, using a step ladder, marked the stud to length where it hit the string line. I then cut each 2×4 on that mark with a handsaw and nailed it in place with four toe nails to the bottom plate. (A toe nail is one driven in at an angle rather than straight.) It took us about six months to frame the house. I and two other carpenters have framed many a house in two days!

Once the studs were cut to length and nailed in place at the bottom, the top plate was nailed to the upright studs (again, from a step ladder) and strengthened with a double top plate. The fin-

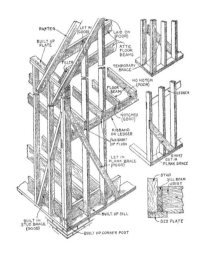

Balloon framing.

> **"Time doesn't fly by for us. It stays. We are the ones to go."**

ished wall averaged about 8 ft. 6 in. in height. With the first wall built, you could move on to the next until all the outside and inside walls were upright.

The walls were then braced to stay plumb by nailing blocks between the studs at an angle from the bottom plate to the top plate. This is a good, solid, bracing system as long as a wall has two braces running diagonally in opposition to each other. The problem is that the blocks had to be cut on the angle with a handsaw, which took considerable time and effort. But then, maybe those carpenters were in less of a rush than we modern people. In the words of Austin Dobson (1877), "Time doesn't fly by for us. It stays. We are the ones to go."

THE TOOLS IN 1900 were pretty much the same as those I used in the 1930s and even in 1950. The ubiquitous framing square was the tool of choice to lay out rafters for the roof. The pitch or slope on our old house must have been about 4 in 12. This means that for every foot that a rafter moved toward the center of the house, it rose 4 in., giving the roof its characteristic slope. Every rafter was laid out with a framing square, cut to length on the ground, and then nailed in place on top of the walls alongside each ceiling joist and to the ridge board at the peak. The rafters were then sheathed with 1×12 boards and covered with tar paper.

The wood roof shingles were from cedar trees. They too must have come from the huge, old-growth cedar trees that were found in the Pacific Northwest. Like the fir and the spruce, most of these cedar trees are history. Powerful, giant timber companies had them brought down with their chainsaws and sent to their lumber mills. Do you ever wonder how the way we treat our earth and its resources will affect our children? Has mass consumerism pushed

The big trees were out on the West Coast by the millions. They were brought out of the forest a few at a time to the mills until only a few remained.

the envelope too far? Is the day of reckoning at hand? Should we just "eat, drink, and be merry" and to hell with tomorrow?

There was, I am told, a sustainable, mixed-growth forest here in the Northwest. Some people look at a forest and see board feet and dollar signs. Others look and see a vibrant, living system on which many, many creatures, including us, depend for life.

Most of these extensive forests that had stood for centuries were clear-cut in the span of 30 years or so after World War II. Clear-cutting means that every tree is brought low with no regard for animals, birds, or fish (most often salmon and steelhead), allowing their spawning grounds to be clogged with run-off dirt from the steep hillsides. Once a section of forest is logged off, the limbs are pulled together into piles and burned. What is wrong with this picture? Am I missing something?

Salmon runs up all the rivers and streams were once, not long ago, filled with fish numbering in the millions. Old-timers tell me that they made such a splashing noise when they began their spring or fall run to their spawning beds that you could "hear them coming from a mile away." These huge runs, simply put, no longer exist. Commercial salmon fishing on the West Coast has mainly gone the way of the towering trees. How sad is that?

Nowadays, clear-cut Oregon is pretty much a huge tree plantation of hybrid Douglas firs. A friend here told me that Oregon now has more trees growing than ever before. Maybe true, but is there not a difference between a cathedral and a plantation? I carry in my pickup a small piece of a 2×3 stud that I salvaged from a remodel job. It is a piece of old-growth Douglas fir with 22 growth rings per inch. The fast-growing plantation trees that cover our hills need to be sprayed with pesticides and fertilizer. They have as few as 2 or 3 growth rings per inch!

The size of these old trees was truly unbelievable, as I mentioned before. A friend here in Oregon worked in many mills for 41 years. He said that logs used to come in that were 40 ft. long, 6 ft. to 8 ft. at the base, and only a few inches less at the other end without a branch. He also said that a big portion of these trees was wasted in the milling process. Huge slabs were cut off and sent up in smoke along with mountains of sawdust in the burning wigwam. I came from a culture and a time where every scrap of everything was used and reused. My eyes still widen in disbelief when I see what we send to the landfills without a second thought. Do we really believe, as Robert Earl Keen wrote, that "the road goes on forever and the party never ends"?

The outside of our old house was, fortunately, covered with tar paper, which at least slowed the wind-driven snow down a bit. The walls themselves had zero insulation. Double-hung windows set in wood frames were universally used in most every house. "Double

The lumber mills burned a good part of every tree in wigwam burners.

hung" means that both window frames (sash) were vertically movable. The trouble was that the sash was not weatherstripped. Because they fit rather loosely in the frame, wind whistled in around the edges.

Each year, before winter set in, Mother gave us children strips of cloth and table knives. We were directed to stuff the cloth all the way around the window to close the gap between the sash and the frame. Heavy, thick frost would build up on the single panes, leaving puddles on the sill and floor when it finally melted. I used to push pennies against the frost and leave imprints of Abraham Lincoln in the ice. Even though we had few playthings, I don't recall feeling bored. We invented games, put on skits, sang songs, and danced. Maybe boredom is a modern affliction.

Plywood didn't come into common use until after World War II, so siding was nailed directly to the studs. The siding used on our

There was little money for clothes, let alone for paint. My father, Henry Haun, reading the *Scottsbluff Star Herald* in front of our weather-beaten house.

old house was also made from cedar trees. It was lap siding, often called clapboard. I am not sure that this siding was ever painted, though I do know it never received paint on the outside while we lived there. It certainly was well weathered, like the faces of the old-timers who spent a lifetime working outside for their keep.

The absence of insulation meant that the temperature on the inside of the house was pretty much the temperature outside, especially in the bedrooms. Mother used to iron our sheets with a flat iron heated on the stove. That helped for about 30 seconds as we jumped into bed and pulled the covers over our heads. In the winter, people didn't dare sleep with their heads uncovered lest they wake to find frozen spots on their faces. These days when I crawl into bed I give thanks for the flannel sheets and down covers that keep me warm.

One of the main problems we had keeping warm at night was that we were sleeping on cloth bags stuffed with straw. Two turns on this mattress and you were sleeping on nothing but cloth. The straw didn't stay in place. Help came to town in the form of a New Deal project. Woman gathered in the building of the Knights of Pythias (a fraternal order dedicated to universal peace), where they were supplied with heavy cloth that they stuffed full with 3 in. of cotton that was stitched to stay in place. I now knew what heaven was all about.

The only real heat in the house came from the cast-iron kitchen stove used for cooking, heating bath water, and baking bread. Back in those days, everyone was living "off the grid." Mother was always up at 4 a.m., shaking the ashes down through the grate and laying in kindling to start another fire. The problem was that on cold winter days if you stood 3 ft. away from the stove your front side felt warm but your backside was cold. Turn around to warm your backside and you could see your breath. It was nigh impossible to get warm "all the way through." This house was by no stretch of the imagination energy efficient, but at least we didn't have to worry about the mold and rot that can accumulate in an airtight house.

My mother was an accomplished bread baker, and she made loaves and buns twice a week for her hungry children. The cast-iron cook stove had no temperature gauge to tell her when the heat was high enough to insert the pans of dough that had been rising since early morning. She used to tell the proper temperature for baking by opening the oven door and sticking her arm in to test the heat. Remembering the taste of this warm, fresh-baked bread covered with homemade butter still makes me homesick.

ONCE THE HOUSE FRAME was standing and the outside closed in, work could begin preparing the walls for plaster. There were no plumbing pipes or electrical wires to be installed, slowing down construction. Our inside lighting came from kerosene lamps.

We finally did get a radio powered by a dry-cell battery larger than the radio when I was eight. We were limited to one hour of listening a day. There was no local station, so we tuned into the powerful clear-channel stations like the one from "Del Rio, Texas" on the border with Mexico. We enjoyed listening to the Carter family singing old-time songs. One of my favorites was their version of "Wildwood Flower." How many of us have not shed a tear or two as we listen to the closing lines: "Oh, I long to see her and regret the dark hour/She's gone and neglected her pale wildwood flower?" The ads were there too, of course. We heard that goat testicles would increase a man's virility. Yesterday's Viagra®.

No plumbing meant that we went outside to the ever-present two-holer when "nature called." The toilet, like the cellar, was inhabited by spiders. I was always afraid that a black widow might bite my bare bottom hanging down in the hole. Lacking rolls of toilet paper, it was here that we made use of old issues of the famous Sears® and Roebuck catalog. I say famous, because for me it held pictures of wondrous items that allowed me to dream and to fantasize other worlds. The catalog's warm clothes, fancy dresses for my mother, musical instruments, bicycles, grandfather clocks, and dollar watches were all wonders to me. One drawback: The catalog had a number of slick pages that actually didn't work as well for toilet paper as the soft ones. Enough of that, no?

The grid didn't come to isolated rural areas until after 1936, when Congress passed the Rural Electrification Act. Some farm families were able to purchase a Wincharger® wind turbine along with a cellar full of storage batteries. This 32-volt system allowed them to have a few electric lights, an electric iron, and even a refrigerator. I can't help but wonder where we would be today if this type of electrical generation had been encouraged.

Because there was no electrical power in our rural area, no wires had to be pulled through the wall studs to serve light switches, outlets, and overhead lightbulbs. This left the inside ready for plaster, which was prepped for by covering the walls and ceiling with wood lath. Strips of lath, $3/16$ in. thick, $1\frac{1}{2}$ in. wide, and 32 in. long, were nailed to the ceiling joists and wall studs with small lathing nails. This type of plaster preparation was still common in 1950 and was used on the houses I worked on in California. Once the lath was in place, walls were plastered with three coats of a lime and cement mixture.

THE ROOF WITH ITS WOOD SHINGLES shed rainwater well enough, but not wind-driven snow. There's one story I almost hesitate to tell because it seems unbelievable. The lock on our front door used a skeleton key. When this key was out of the lock, it left a hole about the size of a wood pencil. Wind-driven snow could enter through this small hole. If the wind direction was just right, you might wake in the morning to find a drift inside the house that was the height of the keyhole and 6 ft. long. Pretty amazing! This is something to remember when you are trying to seal a house to make it energy efficient. It doesn't take much of a hole in a wall to allow a tremendous amount of cold air to enter.

A similar thing happened in our attic every time we had a blizzard. Snow found its way through cracks in the shingles. We children were sent up in the attic through the access hole with small shovels or the dust pan. We scooped up the snow and placed it in buckets that were handed down to be taken outside and dumped. Left up there, the snow would melt and cause chunks of plaster to dissolve and fall. Efforts were made to replace old, cracked, windblown shingles. We lived 30 miles from the nearest hardware store and didn't have the money to go there and buy new cedar shingles. So we recycled and salvaged what was available locally. We'd cut the top and bottom out of a tin can and then cut

"Roofs around town took on the look of patchwork quilts."

the can part down the middle, flatten it, and nail the can in place over a hole in the roof. Old car license plates were also commonly put to use for the same purpose. Roofs around town took on the look of patchwork quilts.

Besides her beloved piano that she played for us children while singing old Irish songs, my mother had several other treasures. She had an old-fashioned, rounded-top trunk that held a few photos; a quilt hand sewn by her own mother from neckties; round, beaded necklaces that she wore on her wedding day; and a lace tablecloth with linen napkins that we used only on very special days. We normally covered our table with a piece of oilcloth printed with brightly colored flowers. Oilcloth was made from heavy cotton or linen and given a linseed oil treatment. It is sort of like today's vinyl, but without the polyvinyl chloride. These items held memories for my mother, but (other than her children) were not her most important treasure.

This treasure came as a gift from my father in about 1938. I remember well the expression on Mother's face when he came in the door carrying a pressure cooker. What a gift for someone having to "put up" food so her family could eat during the winter months! Up until that time, canning—preserving food—was done mainly in a water bath. Jars of food were put into water and boiled until they became sealed. Badly sealed food could spoil and be poisonous to eat. Preserving foods with a pressure cooker is faster, safer, and took less fuel to keep the kitchen stove blazing. The one my mother had held eight pint jars or four quarts. During the harvest months it was on the stove steaming away around the clock.

Snow wasn't the only thing that worked its way into our house. In the Dirty 30s, or the Dust Bowl days, "black blizzards" rolled across the plains states from Texas to Nebraska. These wind storms blotted out the sun, turning day into night. (Our chickens

Sunday April 14, 1935
Dust Clouds Rolling Over the Prairies
Storall Studio Dodge City, Kansas #5

Dust storms—"black blizzards"—were deadly. As the saying goes, "They were not healthy for children and other living things."

would go back to the hen house believing nighttime had come.) The storms were carrying dust from millions of acres of valuable topsoil from land that should never have been plowed and planted in the first place. You could see the blizzard coming from miles away from the south, unlike the white blizzards that came mainly from the north. Before they arrived, Mother would soak bed sheets, flour sacks, or other cloth in water and hang them wet over every window and door in the house. She had us children wrap our faces with a wet, cloth flour sack and stay in a room on the lee side. All this helped, but once the dusty blow was over, days were spent removing dirt that seemed to pay no attention to the wet sheets. This was the time of a massive migration of people abandoning their homesteads and heading California way, as recorded in *The Grapes of Wrath* by John Steinbeck.

To replace a broken window pane was costly for Depression-era people. Hail, at times larger than big marbles, was feared for a number of reasons. Hailstones could be deadly to chickens that didn't have the sense to "get in out of the rain," strip all the leaves from veggies growing in the garden and crops in the fields, and batter and break shingles on the roof. The few cars in the area had small dents in their metal tops. I heard stories about a field of wheat my father was harvesting. It was making about 40 bushels to the acre when a hailstorm arrived and put an end to that project. If a hailstorm came with wind, a stone could easily break a window pane. Mother's remedy for this was to have us children hold pillows against the panes on the inside to soften the blow of a hailstone hitting from the outside.

ONE OF THE HIGHLIGHTS of my early life was to help my mother in her garden, which was right near the windmill. She loved to garden. When I think of her planting seeds in soil made rich with compost, she reminds me of a character played by Geraldine Page in a film called *The Trip to Bountiful.* In the film, Geraldine returns to her old home, goes to the back of her house, kneels down and picks up handfuls of earth, and lets it run through her fingers. My mother was like that, respecting and caring for the earth that helped her raise good food for her children.

I remember seeing a bumper sticker: "Save the earth, it is the only planet that has chocolate." Beyond that, it is the only planet we have. If we can slow down for just a minute, we know that our very lives depend upon how we treat our home, Mother Earth. My mother knew this. She knew the land was sacred and would have been appalled to see how often we mistreat this earth that gives us life.

Times do change, but not necessarily for the better. We do have more things, but do we have more happiness? I was born at a time and in a place where no one had electricity, people talked to each other face to face because there was no radio, TV, or telephone. I used a telephone for the first time when I was 13 years old. I remember trying to figure out how to hold it to speak into the right end. I learned about the world and life by listening to stories told on porches, at work, and at the dinner table. As Stuart Kestenbaum wrote, "Bless our stories that they may somehow be true, for this is all we have." Yes, this really is all we have.

Really, what else do we have other than our stories? Everything else comes and goes, but our stories remain. They tell us why we are here. They keep us from cynicism and despair, reminding us that the way things are is not at all permanent. We don't have to continue to race madly to use up every available resource, exhausting ourselves and Mother Earth. Our stories tell us that there is a better, richer, more uplifting, and sustainable way to live. It doesn't have to be a dog-eat-dog world. People can and do come together for the common good.

I have a friend who tells me that we are all "hard-wired to care." He says that because of this, it is in helping and serving others that we find real happiness. This, if true, puts the lie to the bumper sticker that says, "He who dies with the most toys wins." It lets us know that even though we win the rat race, we may still be a rat.

We see this caring in the tough economic times of today. Stories are told when a disaster happens: Katrina, 9/11, a tsunami, a tornado, or an earthquake. We hear tell of sadness and heartaches, but also of a more human way of being. People lay down their iPods and come together, bonded by a basic goodness, reaching out to victims with food, clothing, care, and love. Police, firemen, and ordinary citizens risk life and limb to help fellow human beings.

We hear about how people set aside their fears, narrow views, and political and religious differences and open their hearts to alleviate suffering in ways that they can. These are stories of hope, courage, and compassion. These are stories about what is important to uplift our hearts and spirits. They give us life. They inspire us to go on for another day and to take one more step into the unknown. 🌺

"I've been havin' some hard travelin',
I thought you knowed."

—Woody Guthrie, "HARD TRAVELIN'"

CHAPTER FOUR

The Dugout

DUGOUTS, LITTLE MORE THAN holes in the ground, were still around until I was in my teens. I used to visit an old man who lived in one when I was out riding my beloved pinto horse. I was working for a rancher, looking for some of his cows that might have strayed down along the White River. The old man's name was Charley, and up until the late 1940s he lived in a home dug back into a bank along this river. He lived alone and worked now and then for ranchers cleaning chicken coops, painting a shed, fixing fences. This gave him a little money for food. His rent was free.

I got to know him some over a period of several months, always stopping by to say hello. One day he invited me in for a cup of coffee. In the West, you don't refuse that kind of an offer no matter who it comes from. Once my eyes became accustomed to the darkness, I saw that his place measured about 10 ft. by 10 ft. His table and chairs were tree rounds cut from a nearby cottonwood. His bed was

"My very first memory as a child is from 1934 when I was three years old."

a pile of rags in a corner. On the small iron stove sat a tea kettle, a frying pan, and a coffee pot. The orange-crate cabinet held a few dishes. He reached for a couple of cups, wiped them out with another rag, and poured us each a hot cup of coffee.

I could feel his loneliness as he told me part of his story. He used to be a painter living in San Francisco with a woman who "did him wrong." I never had the chance to get the woman's side of the story. Once she left, he drifted north, living in Washington and then Montana for a time. And now here he was, heartbroken, living out his days in a place little better than a rabbit hole. He showed me a couple of figures, cowboys on horses, he had drawn with charcoal on butcher paper. I held them to the light and gave him praise. He died that fall when I was back in school. They buried him on the prairie far from any kin, another unknown resting in a different type of dugout.

I never told my mother I visited him in his place. If he had bedbugs, they must have preferred his blood to mine and, lucky for me, I didn't bring any home.

MY VERY FIRST MEMORY as a child is from 1934 when I was three years old. We went on a springtime picnic to Pumpkin Creek, which ran along the Wildcat Hills to the north of our town. These hills separated the upland plains from the fertile North Platte River valley below. What I saw and heard there has remained with me these many years later. Male redwing blackbirds were hanging on cattail reeds, staking out their territory, and singing their mating song.

It's another one of those fading opportunities: If you haven't heard and seen these beautiful birds with their red wing patches and uplifting song, I heartily recommend you take the time to do so. They really only show their striking color and sing their song in the springtime. Just like us, they put on their fine clothes and sing as they go a-courting. They announce their readiness to find a mate by showing their bright red patches and singing their distinctive song.

Sadly, you will have to go somewhere other than Pumpkin Creek to see the redwings. What was once a healthy, clear-water stream full of frogs, trout, and other creatures is no more. Some folk say that the powerful, center-pivot irrigation wells have dropped the water level in the aquifer and dried up this creek. It went the way of many other streams in our agricultural states.

Yes, I feel sad about this isolated local stream, but it is but a tiny part of a global sadness that grips me from time to time. It comes at times when I feel overwhelmed by what is happening to Mother Earth and those of us who live here. I find solace by going to my garden and getting my hands in the soil, preparing it for springtime seeds. Then each year when the sun returns and begins to warm the earth, I gratefully plant the seeds I have been guarding. Maybe we should stop for a moment, have a cup of tea together, and give thanks that we are here and able to plant one more season. I like to remember though, that even if I live to be a hundred I will only have seen a hundred planting seasons.

The sadness is there, yes, and I have found it important not to back off from it, but rather to embrace it as part of life. To play like it isn't there doesn't seem helpful. Once, years ago now, I took time to look at some of the sources of sadness (see the next page):

Sources of Sadness

Glimpses of sadness come in those between spaces,
The drifty times between awake and sleep.
Special things happen there,
A time that is neither good nor bad, just there.

First comes the sadness of being human,
A genetic sadness, the sister of joy they say.
It lies deep within each tender heart,
Neither good nor bad, just there.

Then comes the longing sadness,
Of wanting to be with you.
This is a crazy-making sadness,
Neither good nor bad, just there.

A being lonely sadness drifts in next,
Coming from those long ago, shy times.
I talk about it now recalling the joy of meeting,
Being neither good nor bad, just there.

The being left sadness is never far away,
A deep, wandering sadness.
Marked by children gone, lovers lost,
Still neither good nor bad, just there.

The last sadness comes from seeing butterflies, rainbows, flowers,
For only one life is given to us, one small, short life.
Not long now until you and I and the next one are beyond all this,
Strange, not even this is good or bad, just there.

TAKE A LOOK AT the photo of the dugout on the facing page.
In the background, you can see the sandstone cliffs of the Wildcat
Hills where we went for our annual spring picnic. Not far away from
our picnic grounds was this dugout shelter built and occupied by
early settlers. I have been told that Lee Dozier, the homesteader, is

This dugout in western Nebraska must have been for bachelors only.

the man seated in front of the entrance to his home. To the right is a young botanist, Dr. Pool, with his collection bag, who spent the summer of 1905 studying plant life and gathering specimens from the western part of the state for study at the University of Nebraska in Lincoln, nearly 500 miles to the east.

There are those who say that nothing is permanent, that everything is changing all the time. My experience tells me that this is true, with one exception. In western Nebraska, the seasons come and go, the bright sun gives way to the darkened night, people are born and die, but the wind never stops. Some days it blows with a gentleness that can cool the hot summer nights. Other days it blows with a ferocity that can push empty railroad cars from the tracks, uproot trees, and cover houses with driven snow piled many feet deep.

"In western Nebraska the seasons come and go, the bright sun gives way to the darkened night, people are born and die, but the wind never stops."

It's hard to think of a better place to locate wind turbines to generate electricity. There is no shortage of wind and lots of open land. And each year there are fewer habitants as we move to the cities. Seeking what? There is a problem though: A major flyway for migrating birds comes right through this area. The winged ones that fly low to the ground, especially at night, can't see the whirling propellers. Thousands are killed every year. But these wind turbines give us electricity in our houses. Turn on the TV please and let's watch *Jeopardy!*

Now we didn't need to be a weatherman to know all this about the wind. All we had to do was step outside, hold on to our hats, place a wet finger upright and feel it cool off, or freeze, from the blast of an Old Blue North'rn that started first in the frozen parts of Canada. More often it was heard that it was another "ill wind blowing no good" coming to us clear from the North Pole.

Because of these strong winds, the old-timers had a saying: "Build low to the ground if you want to survive a Nebraska winter." The dugout, a cousin to the soddy (see Chapter 1), is testament that some people listened to this advice. In many ways the dugout was more adapted to the harsh weather than the sod house. Like a gopher, a badger, or a prairie dog comfy in an underground burrow, dwellers in dugouts were protected from that bitter wind that blew down across the snow-covered sagebrush hills of Wyoming and into western Nebraska.

I find it amazing that these earth dwellers never hopped a freight train and headed south. Why did they stay put? Is it not easier to be poor in sunny southern California than in the frozen hills of the high plains? Many stayed because they had no means or money to move on. Others hesitated to leave friends and family.

Still others stayed because they remembered that after the harsh winter came the shocking beauty of the prairie in full springtime bloom, calm moonlit nights, and a silence that healed the soul.

THE PARENTS OF MY CHILDHOOD PLAYMATES, Hester and Ed Stockton, built and lived in one of these holes, a dugout, their prairie home. The story I heard is that they came to Harrisburg in the 1920s from Montana. Ed was able to find enough work to allow them to rent a house, purchase a Model T Ford, and buy food and clothing for themselves and their children. They were surviving until the Crash came in 1929, another failure of our free-enterprise system that left huge numbers of people out of work and hungry.

Bib overalls on Brother Joe and me in 1935. They never seem to go completely out of style.

Having lived from the Great Depression to the Great Recession, I sometimes get asked if times were tougher in the 1930s. Well, in my experience, they definitely were. In my early days, there was little protection built into our system to help working people. There was no Social Security check coming in every month, no pension check for long-time workers, no unemployment compensation, no food stamps, and little or no access to health care. People did what we always do in tough times. We helped each other out, sharing what we had until better economic times came round. Those better times did show up, but not until 12 years later in 1941, with the beginning of World War II. Is war the only door to prosperity?

I look at children today going to school with torn and patched jeans. That's the style, and who would think of being "out of style"? Bib overalls, with patches on patches, were our daily wear. At least we had food to eat. Blessed be our mother!

Every town seems to have an old building or two it tries to preserve to help us remember our past.

Life in those tough Depression times really was hard. Unlike today, class distinctions were practically nonexistent. Everyone I knew was poor, struggling to keep food on their tables and clothes on their backs.

Hard times then and now seem to breed two types of people. Some become more generous, willing to share what little they have. Others seem obsessed with finding someone to blame for their troubles. Sound familiar? It was during the 1930s that there was a big resurgence of Ku Klux Klan activity all across the prairie states. What do you do when there are no Jews or Blacks around as the focal point for your frustration and hatred? That's an easy one. We were the only Catholic family in the entire county.

What happened from all this is a powerful childhood memory that I can now look upon as a gift, a blessing. I was near five years old when some of our neighbors burned a cross in front of our home. I was scared, hiding behind my mother's skirt. At school, my brothers and sisters were taunted as "cat-licks." Then came the day when several men, clothed in the white cloth of the Klan with their pointed hats and mounted on horses, rode around our house.

During the cross burning and later on the ride-around, another neighbor, Jack Mercer, stood by my parents' side shouting out the names of every rider. He recognized them, hidden behind their sheets, by their horses, their shoes, or their stature. This was, after all, a small community where everyone knew everyone. So instead of being forever laden with fear or hatred, I was gifted with the knowledge of the integrity and courage it takes to stand up in the face of racism, sexism, or other adversity. Jack set a standard for how I have tried to live my own life.

Once the KKK riders left, several of them went to a small coffee shop not six blocks from our house. Mother, so I am told, rolled up an issue of the *Scottsbluff Star-Herald* and marched over to the café. She grabbed one of them by the collar, jerked him from his

What's left of the old café where Mother worked over a local Klan member with a rolled-up newspaper.

chair, and gave him a few whacks across the face with her rolled-up newspaper. Never mess with a mother guarding her children!

Even though dugouts were quite warm and cozy inside, they carried a stigma. The stigma, of course, is one that often comes with being poor. People living in frame houses, the bigger the better, are just from a higher class. We all know that! Unfortunately, that kind of thinking persists to this day. Ask yourself how you think about your neighbors living up there on the hilltops or down there beyond the railroad tracks. Why don't those lazy bums just find a job and go to work instead of living off welfare? In the meantime, I am told, "The rich get much richer, the poor are getting poorer, and the middle class are left sucking hind tit," as they say in the Midwest, referring to the smallest suckling in a batch of piglets.

I recall a discussion I had with a person in an airport after Hurricane Andrew hit Florida in 1992. I casually asked him if anything was left of the place where he lived. He answered, "Our big house still stands strong. The hurricane blew away all the riff-raff along with their shacks and trailer parks." Let's hear it for hurricanes!

UNTIL JOBS OPENED UP during wartime, people scraped together a few dollars any way they could. One way that some survived was as a result of our government's efforts to control—read eradicate—the coyote. In some parts of our country, coyotes are hated as much as wolves and rattlesnakes. It's true, they can do serious damage to a herd of sheep or a flock of chickens, but it seems legitimate to ask if the "coyote problem" would have existed at all if we hadn't exterminated their natural enemy, the wolf. Why do we think that we know more about how the natural world should be run than nature itself? Where does this urge to control everything around us come from? There is a balance in nature. Destroy this balance and pay the price. I have witnessed times without coyotes when rabbits and rodents became so numerous that crop and grain losses were substantial.

To favor sheep raisers and other coyote haters, the government offered a bounty in the 1930s: Bring in the ears of a coyote to the county agent and receive $1.00. That $1.00 was often more than the going daily wage for people when they were fortunate enough to find work during the Great Depression. This war on coyotes has been going on for decades and has cost millions and millions of taxpayer dollars to kill millions of coyotes. They are killed by any means necessary: shot from helicopters, poisoned with cyanide, captured with steel traps, and asphyxiated in their dens. But guess what? The "trickster" won. Coyotes used to be mainly west of the Mississippi. Now they are in 49 states and much of Canada and

Mexico, laughing at us. I have seen them in many places in Los Angeles, loping through the parks and streets with that crooked smile on their face.

THE MAIN TOOLS NEEDED to build a dugout shelter are a shovel, a strong back, and determination. Our neighbor Ed Stockton and his family couldn't pay the rent on their wood-frame home so they had to move on around 1930. A rancher allowed them to build a dugout on a "worthless" piece of ground about two miles outside our town. They picked out a south-facing hillside, bent over, and started digging.

Worthless land often meant that access to water was limited. The old saying, "Never look a gift horse in the mouth," water or no water, seems to apply here: Take what is given to you. The Stockton family sometimes hauled their water from our well in town. Limited water meant limited bathing, even for my family. Saturday afternoon was bath time for us, willing or not. Mother heated water on the kitchen stove, poured it into a round clothes-washing tub, and one by one, starting with the oldest first, we cleaned our bodies. The water was not changed for each bather. Each of us had a bucket full to rinse off after bathing in the "used" water. This type of bathing was known as "giving yourself a lick and a promise." At least we all, from oldest to youngest, smelled pretty much the same. We had yet to see the soap advertisement that reassures customers, "You can have that sporty look without the sporty smell." Lord, yes, spare us from that sporty smell!

My mother often gave the Stocktons flour as well, precious flour. That, with a little lard, salt, water, and sourdough yeast, was turned into our staple—bread. Not only was flour treasured, but the fact that it came in 50-lb. cloth bags was something special. These sacks were highly prized and turned into items most of us hardly think about today. They were cut, hemmed, and sewn on the ever-present, treadle-operated Singer sewing machine. Diapers for children, towels to dry dishes, sanitary napkins, and even pieces of clothing like pajamas came from this cloth.

TODAY, WE HAVE A FANCIER NAME for dugouts: "earth-sheltered homes." Does this help remove the stigma? There are lots of reasons to live down under. Heating and cooling costs are minimal, pipes don't freeze, tornadoes and hurricanes blow right over you, and you can plant a garden on your roof. The main problem with this type of construction is that these days it is not for the poor. Initial costs, so I understand, are at least 20 percent higher than building above ground. But, if you have the money, you can lean on your shovel and watch the hole being dug with a back hoe and a skip loader and the dirt hauled away in a dump truck.

An early "earth-sheltered home" in our small village.

We had a number of earth-sheltered homes in our village, an upgrade from a hole dug back into a bank. People with a little money dug a basement into the ground, poured concrete walls, and covered the structure with a flat roof. The entryway was built above ground. They were definitely warmer in the winter than in an above-ground frame house.

You have to stick your shovel in the ground a lot of times to excavate a room about 12 ft. deep and 30 ft. long, the size of our playmates' home, but that's what they did. Shovel after shovel was loaded into a wheelbarrow and wheeled away to become a dirt pile where we children played. Walls were scraped straight and clean, leaving a room with 360 sq. ft. of living space.

As children we spent many days playing on our friends' front lawn, the endless prairie. We wandered the hills looking for treasures, rattlesnakes, wild fruit, and signs that Native Americans had once lived there. We ran footraces, did somersaults, and wrestled in the grasses. We built forts from tumbleweeds and sagebrush, hiding behind them and pretending that we were ready to meet the enemy. We dug our own underground rooms and covered them with whatever we could scrounge: wood scraps, old metal signs, and sagebrush. I didn't understand the extent of their, or our, poverty until years later. I felt free to just be. No one ever wanted me to be other than who I was. As the bumper sticker says, "Be yourself. Everyone else is taken." I was left to just be myself. I give thanks for that gift.

Even without TV, Playstations®, Xboxes®, and iPods, we children always had creative ways to enjoy each other and our lives, costing nothing but our time. One day my sisters, Margaret and Loretta, decided to hang brother Joe and me out to dry on our clothesline. What fun! I remembered this in a poem from years ago:

Flapping in the Breeze on #9 Wire

Wyoming wind blowing too hard for kites,
So what's a big sister to do?
Let's hang a couple of kid brothers
On the clothesline.

Winter-killed line sagging like a sway-back horse.
Stand straight with your arms out!
Twenty clothespins to the shirt on each arm.
Raise them high like a ridge beam.
Get that center post under the line.
Flapping in the breeze on #9 wire.

I remember it,
Not just the old photo,
But I remember.
Springtime, sunshine,
Brother and I, hanging on #9 wire.
Flapping in the breeze like a Monday shirt.

What children did before they had an iPod or even a telephone.

My father with Tiny, our Jersey cow, who gave us growing children fresh, rich milk.

The dirt walls remained dirt walls. How could they be different? The only plaster available was mud made from the excavated dirt. Sometimes a white sheet would be hung over a wall section to lighten the space a bit. I recall seeing niches dug into their back wall where the Stocktons could set a kerosene lamp or maybe a prairie flower in a quart jar. Yes, even the poor like flowers.

Often the front wall section of a dugout was constructed much like a soddy, with strips of sod piled up to form a wall. Our friends' front wall was different. They set posts in the ground about every 6 ft. to hold an overhead roof pole. Around the posts they wrapped chicken wire on both sides. The space between the posts was then stuffed full of hay and dirt excavated from the hillside.

We actually had a similar outbuilding at home that looked like a hay stack when finished. It was a small space, maybe 6 ft. by 10 ft., that housed our Jersey milk cow, Tiny, when the weather was bad. It was a simple type of construction, but adequate to offer her some protection from the icy cold in the winter months.

Our friends' south-facing front wall had a door and two small windows. From somewhere they had acquired a few rough boards that they nailed together to form a door. It was held to the door frame by leather hinges, strips of heavy leather nailed to the door and to the jamb. To open the door, you actually had to pick it up first and then swing it outward. No lock needed on this door.

The window panes were not real glass. People had devised a way to let in a little light by using what was called butcher paper. This paper was white or light tan and came in a large, 2-ft.-wide roll. It was used in grocery stores to wrap fresh meat for a customer. To make a window pane, the first step was to cut a window-frame-size piece from this paper. Then the paper was coated on both sides with tallow, lard rendered from animal fat. This gave some strength and durability to the paper, which was then secured to the frame. Not much light entered through these makeshift panes, but as the saying goes, it was better than nothing.

Until electricity came to this area in the 1940s, inside light was provided by candles and kerosene lamps. These lamps had a cotton wick that drew kerosene up from a bowl container. Once the wick was lit, a glass chimney was placed over it for protection and to diffuse the light from the flame. The wick could be moved up or down. Now and then it needed to be trimmed with a scissors so it would burn evenly. My parents had a beautiful silver lamp with a round wick that produced enough light so we could study, play card games, and do puzzles at the kitchen table during the winter months.

WE HAD ANOTHER NEIGHBOR that all of us children used to visit. His name was Bill Zorn and he kept us in awe with his stories. He was an old-time buffalo hunter. It was only years later that I learned what this meant: He had been hired by the U.S. Army with the explicit charge to kill as many buffalo as he could. That's right, just kill them. Quite a tall order, considering that an estimated 50 to 60 million buffalo occupied the Great Plains before the coming of the European settlers. By 1885 only 2,000 buffalo, more or less, were left, mainly in Yellowstone Park. The hunters had done their job well. As a boy, wandering the hills and valleys, I used to find numerous buffalo skulls scattered about, the last vestige of this grand animal to decay.

Philip Sheridan was one of the main generals on the Union side in America's Civil War. It was his driving force that brought about the defeat of his Confederate brothers. He was also quite active in the Indian Wars that erupted in 1867 when Major Chivington massacred a large group of peaceful Indians at Sand Creek in Colorado. General Sheridan is the one who infamously said, "Let them kill, skin, and sell until the buffalo is exterminated, as it is the only way to bring lasting peace and allow civilization to advance." This, of course, put the Native people who had lived on their now-coveted land for centuries among the uncivilized. Killing their food and source of clothing would keep them on the reservations, dependent on others for the basics of life. Is this what civilized

The home of an old buffalo hunter. It was off-limits to us children, as Mother feared it harbored bedbugs.

people do? Destroy the livelihood and culture of others so
they and their resources can
be controlled as we populate
their lands. Why did we have

nothing to learn from these Native people, who had been living on
this land for thousands of years?

Bill used to show us his long buffalo gun with its octagon-
shaped barrel. We weren't allowed to go into his meager house
because Mother suspected that he had bedbugs. She didn't want
us bringing bugs into her home. He died in mid-winter in about
1938. Not a good time to die. How do you bury someone when the
ground is frozen solid to a depth of 4 ft. or 5 ft.? My older brother,
Jim, helped dig the grave. They started by building a bonfire on
the gravesite, heated the ground a bit, and then dug down a few
inches. Heat and dig, until they finally came to unfrozen ground,
allowing them to plant old Bill in his very own dugout.

The roof of a dugout was like that of many of the soddies: Poles
were laid from a beam in the front to the dirt in back. This was covered with tar paper, sagebrush, grasses, and finally dirt taken from
the excavation. It never happened to my friends, but I heard tales
about cows wandering out on the roof of a ground-level dugout and
winding up with legs sticking down into the living room. I wonder
who was more shocked by this, the cow or the people in the dugout.

I was somewhat envious of how warm it always felt inside the
Stocktons' earth-covered home, even in the dead of winter. And
even though they were poorer than poor, they didn't seem to be
unhappy. Ed knew how to play chords on an old battered guitar, a
banjo with one string missing, and could even play a tune on his
harmonica. I always had fun there, singing and dancing around.
Besides that, they all seemed to like each other. I never recall any
quarreling among them. Over the years it has made me think about

what is needed to be happy. I learned that our lives can be materially impoverished but enriched by connection to each other, our family, and the natural world of puffy clouds, bright blue skies, moonlit nights, and wild prairie roses.

The prairie rose especially was treasured. It came in pale colors, yellow, pink, white, often with just five petals. The blossoms were hearty, but transient. Like us they are "here today, gone tomorrow." Cultivated roses were few and far between in Harrisburg. People were more concerned about survival than planting roses. As a small boy, one of my tasks assigned by my tough but gentle mother was to pick up the mail on days it came into town. I went to the small, one-room post office, got the mail, and when I came out the door there it was. A small bush just outside that was blessed with a single white rose. Now what young boy wouldn't want to bring a flower home to his mother?

My mother loved flowers even though, other than cosmos, she had few in her garden. When I handed the white rose to her, instead of joy in her face, I was met with questions: Where did you get that rose? Did you ask permission from the postmistress to pick it? This was followed by the admonition: I know you wanted to please me, but you have to return the rose and tell her that you are sorry for picking it. It is not right to take things from others without their permission! I can still feel the heat that flooded my face when I reentered the post office, head bowed, and handed over the flower. Here, I'm sorry I picked your white rose.

WE MOVED ON to another town in 1942, but I still miss my childhood playmates and their sheltering dugout. I miss other things, too. I miss the sandstone hills where we played in the quiet valleys full of flowers and wild, sweet-tasting berries. Those hills were known to me as only children can know them. They spoke to

my heart, bringing me peace, reminding me that I am not a stranger
in my own world. I miss the rolling
waves of the tall, prairie grasses,
often wild and free. I used to lie back

> "I miss the sandstone hills where we played in the quiet valleys full of flowers and wild, sweet-tasting berries."

flat among them, protected, feeling the summer breeze blowing over my head, letting the grass stems caress me, leaving me feeling safe and cared for.

In the fall of the year, I loved to watch the leaves fall from the few trees we had in our town. They came from their places on branches to blanket our earth with their gold and reddish colors. They waved like unfurled flags as they drifted toward the ground. They reminded me that I, too, am tied to a branch that will one day let me go. 🦋

"Someone someday will trace the roots of modern human loneliness to a loss of intimacy with place, to our many breaks with the physical Earth . . . Human beings long for a specific place, a certain geography that gives them a sense of well-being . . . I strive, when I travel, to meet the land as if it were a person. I wait for it to speak. And wait. And wait."

—Barry Lopez, *NATIONAL GEOGRAPHIC*

CHAPTER FIVE

The Precut House

MODERN HOME No. 165

IT ALWAYS AMAZES ME that we Americans are so restless, always on the move. Sometimes I wonder where it comes from, this restlessness. Like an old prospector, we seem to know that the "mother lode" is just over the next hill. One more grubstake and happiness will be found. So from the covered wagon heading west to our automobiles heading in all directions, we are a people on the go. Like the pioneers, we can load all we want, labeled and tied in boxes and bundles, in a U-Haul®, fold our tent, and move on.

There can be joy in this as we lighten the load, leaving behind excess baggage that has been weighing us down. Old photos show how the early settlers scattered a river of possessions along their

Hundreds of thousands of our ancestors traveled this dusty trail on a 2,000-mile trek to Oregon and California.

trails as they struggled to get to Oregon or California. We, on the other hand, dump our mountain of excess into the trash or cart it off to a thrift store and heave a big sigh: "Free at last, free at last."

I have at times pondered whether it is patriotic to buy things we don't need. Our small, isolated planet does have finite resources. What will we do when the "well runs dry," as my elders used to ask? Environmental problems won't be solved if our main effort in life is to buy more things that no one really needs.

The sad part is that what we lose when we move is not stuff but our sense of place and, more often than not, close contact with our children and their children. I know I miss that. My prairie home nurtured me and let me know who I am in a way that 50 years of city living could never do.

IN 1942, WHEN I WAS ELEVEN, we moved about 100 miles farther north to another isolated rural village, Harrison (pop. 500). This town was not far from the borders of Wyoming and South Dakota and from what was left of the great Lakota nation. The Lakota had been forcibly removed from their beloved Black Hills to a desolate region called the Pine Ridge Reservation. My father had another job working on a New Deal agriculture program that paid a bit more than his previous job as county clerk, but still less than $100 per month. My parents had lost their house in Harrisburg because they were unable to repay a loan of $600 borrowed from the bank to pay for my eldest sister's appendectomy. From then until their deaths, except for a couple of years in Montana, they were renters.

It was here in this cattle-raising outpost that I was introduced to the precut house. We'll get to that in a minute, but first a few words about the trip north to Harrison. It was exciting for me to see new places along the way, but the journey in my parents' Chevrolet® sedan was otherwise uneventful. They had acquired the car in 1929. My father had an accident on a icy road when he was working at a sugar factory in Gering, tipping the car on its side and breaking a window. Winter travel in the old Chevy was cold with or without a broken window, and I was thankful that we made our 100-mile trip in the fall.

My parents sold the car when they settled in the new town and went without a car for many years. It was at this time that I acquired my lifelong love of walking and running, as this was my

Brother Joe and myself, with our pet chicken, cat, and dog, taking a break before our trip north to Harrison.

This is what's left of our home in Harrison, Nebraska. It was, in reality, an oversize refrigerator. A house on a high, windy hill in western Nebraska would have been better built with zero windows.

only way to get around. When we came into our village, I recall seeing a young boy like me standing on a corner smoking a cigarette. That was a bit of a shock. Smoking at that age was a cultural taboo unless you were sneaking a cigarette out behind the barn. He later turned out to be a classmate in school.

I have often wondered why my father, a gentle person, never moved to a more populous town with better job opportunities. My feeling is that he had wounds from World War I that held him back. Not physical wounds, but like many combat vets, deeper experiences that injure the heart. He spoke little of the warfare in France except that "the trenches were filled with mud and blood." We now lived in real-life cowboy country, where guns were an everyday reality. But he wanted nothing to do with any weapon.

There was no construction going on in our new village at the time we arrived. The old house we moved into had been built many years before. To our great joy, it had electricity, running water, indoor toilets, and a place for my mother's beloved garden. A couple of years later, we had a telephone. What a miracle!

This "little house on the prairie" was by no means a green building. It must have been built on the highest spot in all Nebraska. What were they thinking about? A totally uninsulated house with no weatherstripping and way too many single-glazed windows built so the full force of every Wyoming wind could hit it broadside. As the saying goes, carry rocks in your pockets walking in a Wyoming wind.

Like most ranch-farm children, I went to work at an early age. In those days, child labor laws were not well known or practiced in western Nebraska. My first job was at our small grocery store, the Harrison Cash Grocery, at age 11 for the proverbial $1.00 per day. I worked there two summers and after school as a stock boy, moving

Our small grocery store buried under a blizzard. Before the advent of processed food, large stores were scarce. The shelves were filled with what we needed, not what we have been taught to want.

up to cutting meat and even tending the cash register. It was there that I had my first encounter with processed food called by the brand name "Wonder® Bread." The store owner showed me how you could squeeze a long loaf of this bread down to 2 in. or 3 in., release it, and let it come back to full size. Truly a wonder! Processed food had arrived in the back country. I guess it's not news to know I still have a preference for real bread. Even babies are smarter than we are. Feed them this Styrofoam® bread and they make a face and spit it back out.

At age 14, I was hired on as a ranch hand, working with horses and cattle, planting some crops, putting up hay, driving a grain truck without a license, and learning how to operate and repair all kinds of equipment. Picking up a heavy harness and placing it on the back of a big workhorse was almost more than I could do. My left foot still suffers from being stepped on by a restless horse. When I was 16, I got a summer job as a spike driver and gandy dancer (inserting railroad ties beneath the rails and using large spikes to hold them in place) on the now-abandoned Chicago and Northwestern Railroad that ran through our small town. We were working to upgrade the railroad tracks south of town along the beautiful White River, which was full of good-size trout, frogs, and water striders. This union job paid the unheard of sum of 87 cents an hour! For one summer, I was making more than my father. I was able to buy Levi's® jeans for school along with a good pair of shoes.

A good share of my formal education, readin' and writin', came from my mother rather than from school. I did have a good teacher or two, but very few offered any real challenge to my curiosity. I recall going through four years of high school and never being asked to write a paragraph on anything. Sentences yes, but no paragraph! I wasn't a smart alec, just a smart boy who needed some good direction in what to study. Without this, I was often in trouble. Not bad trouble, just doing things a restless boy would do: teasing girls, flying paper kites across the room, shooting paper wads with a rubber band. Most teachers were fairly tolerant of me, except one. He was a big man. Now and then he would pick me up, literally, carry me to the schoolhouse door, and throw me out.

School was not a total waste of my time. I did enjoy taking part in all the sports, I learned how to type in two weeks, and, best of all, I was able to take hot showers in the school basement. Other than that, I often spent time huddled next to the steam radiators trying to stay warm. No texting going on in those days.

My parents allowed me to play hooky a lot. I often skipped days of school and worked on farms and ranches. There I learned the basics of many trades—painting, carpentry, mechanics, welding, cowboying, farming, and ranching—that have served me well. One of my non-school teachers that I worked for and remember fondly

was an old-time rancher, Dan Jordan. He told me tales from when he was a wrangler helping to drive cattle on the open plains from Texas to Montana in the 1800s. This was before the common use of barbed-wire fencing sectioned the land into private property. Bowlegged, he was at home on a horse. He had an old pickup, but never drove in other than second gear, traveling to his different ranches at about the speed a horse could run.

Dan Jordan was a real cowboy from the days when the prairie was wide open and unfenced.

NOW, FINALLY, WE GET TO the subject of this chapter. In 1948, when I was 17, I was working for a country ranch family who had decided to build a precut house for a brother and his family. Up until World War II, thousands and thousands of precut houses were built throughout our country and Canada. These houses were offered in many different models through mail-order catalogs, some costing as little as $1,000.

A precut house, sometimes called a kit house, was just that. Like a set of Lego blocks, it came with all parts cut to size at the factory, packaged, and labeled along with blueprints and many pages of instructions on how to put everything together. These bundles included siding and shingles along with nails, hinges, and other hardware. Nails in those days came in a keg, a small, slatted, wooden barrel held together with iron bands, containing 100 lb. of nails. Plumbing and electrical parts were available, but had to be bought separately.

The house I worked on was ordered through the Sears mail-order catalog. You can still order these houses today, even though their popularity waned radically after World War II. Different styles—bungalow stick frame, timber frame, and log cabins—are all available. In today's version, a set of plans can be programmed into a computer that will instruct automated machinery how to cut all the house parts and even to nail together sections of wall. This approach has value today, especially for the homeowner who wants to save money by being the builder but who doesn't have extensive knowledge of how a house goes together. Further, factory-cut houses help ensure that quality wood is being used and that there is less waste. When these houses are delivered in panels, they go up fast, allowing them to be closed in from the weather pretty rapidly.

The prewar precut house was the forerunner to the revolution in construction that took place in the 1950s, when most of America was on the move and needed housing. Anyone who has spent days on a stack of 2×4s cutting them to stud length with a handsaw knows there has to be a better way. The better way, until we had portable, production circular saws out on the job site, was to cut all the house pieces in a central location. Even when we had power tools, much of what was used in production framing was cut to size at the mill or lumber yard and not on the job site: studs, window and door headers, along with top and bottom cripples, rough sills, blocks, plywood, and roof trusses. These, like a precut house, were bundled and shipped to where we were building.

BEFORE THE HOUSE KIT with its thousands of house parts was brought to the building site, a basement and a foundation had to be dug and concrete poured. There was no backhoe available, so we grabbed our shovels and went to work. Rather than dig back in a hillside for a dugout, we dug down 5 ft. or so for a full, under-house basement. We then built up forms about 2 ft. beyond

Captain John and his son Dee with their team and wagon. Winter or summer, they were available to haul groceries, coal, or materials to your home and take garbage to the city dump.

ground level. All concrete, cement, and sand, moved one shovelful at a time, was readied in an electric mixer and carted to the forms in a wheelbarrow.

Once the basement walls were completed, we mixed "mud" to pour the concrete floor. It was late in the evening as we continued to trowel and finish the newly poured concrete. To shed light on our work, someone handed me a portable, electric "trouble light." It was trouble alright! There was no ground wire to this light, and I was standing in wet shoes on wet concrete. As the shock roared through me, I was hit hard and fell over backward. "Sometimes you get lucky," as the saying goes. The fall pulled the light cord from the socket. That and a young, strong heart allowed me to live to see another day.

The precut house arrived in two rail cars and was set on a siding at the local train depot. From there it was brought, package by package, to the site with a team and wagon operated locally by Captain John and his son Dee, the young boy I saw smoking on the street corner. This is the way the Captain earned his livelihood, carting coal from a railroad car to houses for people's stoves, bringing food to the housebound, and doing general hauling and cleanup around town.

I made it through the electric shock calamity and many other childhood dangers without ever having to seek much medical help. It was just as well. Medical attention was many miles away, especially for us walkers. I did have to go and get a few stitches now and then when I suffered a cut and lost some blood. My parents practiced healing seasonal flu, colds, fevers, and afflictions like measles, mumps, and chickenpox with their prairie herbs, vinegar solutions, mustard hot packs, good food, and love. It seemed to work.

Adolph Eisler, the master carpenter hired to put all the pieces of this house together, was an immigrant from Germany who homesteaded in the county. One of the stories he told was about his first job when he arrived in New York in the 1800s. He found a job helping to make pianos, working for 5 cents an hour. Beer, he said, could be bought for 5 cents a mug. An hour of work bought a mug of beer!

Adolph was my teacher. He came to the job site with his toolbox full of hammers, handsaws, chisels, and wood planes of various sizes that had been handed down to him from his own father. All of his tools, brought over from the "old country," were well oiled, razor sharp, and wrapped in soft cloth to protect them from rust. I could tell that they were sacred to him from the way he used them with utmost care and precision. I was his helper, his apprentice, learning the names of all the tools and all the house parts, bringing them to him as work progressed. What a gift to me. I didn't do a lot of nailing, but the knowledge and work ethic I learned from this patient man are still firmly with me today.

Working in the summertime in the high plains could be quite pleasant. Temperatures at that elevation usually weren't excessive. Neither too hot nor too cold. Sounds like Goldilocks and the Three Bears, no? But summertime also often brought extreme thunderstorms from the west, accompanied by fierce strikes of bolt lightning that made the metal pots and pans dance on our mother's iron kitchen stove. I recall once when I was working on the railroad there was a strike, along with a simultaneous crash of thunder, 3 ft. from me. That ended my workday and left me scared half to death and, once again, grateful to be alive.

Nights were at times lit by what people called "heat lightning," which covered half the eastern sky with flashes of light like a lightbulb being switched on and off in a room. Sometimes, when conditions were right, we would experience the kaleidoscope of color from the northern lights flickering up and down above the horizon.

"Moon dogs," rainbows from moisture in the air highlighted by the light of our moon, added to the night sky. I didn't care for the cold, but I have never regretted growing up in this magical world rather than the paved streets of a crowded city.

It was during these times that my eldest sister Margaret, the kite flyer, the wind lover, the kite book writer, did what older sisters do. She taught me. Her teachings helped me realize that my enemy, the wind, could be seen in different ways; that there are many kinds of winds, not all of them ill. She told me to pay attention to these winds and see what I might learn. Some of what I learned I wrote down.

Sister Teacher Winds

Nothing grows wide in a
Wyoming Wind,
A constant lonely cry—my teacher.

They keep me lean and hungry,
South Coming Winds
Stripping paint from walls, feathers from chickens.

Running north to Bear Butte,
Face Chilling Wind,
Brother with the crazy horse.

Lying back flat in native grasses,
Sky Wind
Paints clouds in wildest circles.

Child wonder surges beyond as
Snow Wind
Drifts across the floor through a keyhole.

"Working is for those who don't know how to fly kites." My oldest sister, Margaret, showing us delight in flying a kite.

Tumbleweeds bounced into our yard by
Wild Wind
Become forts and caves.

Head pulls under covers as
Whistling Wind
Sends corner howls, night long.

It comes now and oftener,
Gentle Wind
Comforting my stepping.

I learn from
Sister Teacher Winds,
Even to love the silence when it stops.

STEP BY STEP, WE PUT ALL THE PARTS

together to frame the house. The bottom plate went down
on the foundation first, followed by floor joists and rim joists,
which were nailed in place and sheathed with 1× stock. Now
and then it was my job to cut a board that didn't quite fit. Walls
with their plates, studs, and headers were assembled, leaving
space for door and window openings. More joists and rafters
formed the ceiling and the roof, which was sheathed and readied for shingles. What a joy to see this whole house rise from the
ground. At the end of the day I could stand back and silently say,
"I helped to do this." It really is a pleasure to be able to work and
create with your own hands. I felt like an artist.

Around this time I received my first real Christmas present. Up
until then presents at Christmas time were fresh, round, sweet-
tasting oranges, clothes we needed for school, extra-good food,
fresh-baked apple pies, and love from my parents. My brother Jim
returned home from the Navy before shipping off to Guam in the

All lined up with big brother Jim before he left for war in the Pacific.

Pacific war. He brought me a real leather football that I used and cherished for many years. How times have changed.

I recently went to a birthday party for a grandson's 13-year-old classmate. It was a rather large, joyful gathering of well-wishers, friends, and relatives celebrating this boy's becoming a teenager. I sat off to the side watching as he opened his gifts. What followed was an unwrapping that shocked my feeling of what children, or any of us for that matter, need. I counted. He opened 37 different gifts, hardly looking at one before grabbing another. A feeling of nausea swept over me. I wanted to hold this boy and tell him that life is not about a pile of presents. Flee for the hills. Get out of town. They will strip-mine your soul. They will clear-cut your heart. "Run for your life!"

Welcome to this coming-of-age rite. It was an initiation showing him what it takes to be happy in our world and putting our blessing on consumerism. Can a society based on how much we buy and consume each day continue to be viable? Somebody pass the Wonder Bread, please.

We sheathed the entire house with 1× stock and then wrapped the house with rolls of tarpaper. The next step, before nailing on the finish siding, was to install the wood-frame windows and door jambs. The siding in this case was a "shingle," 12 in. by 24 in., made from cement mixed with asbestos fibers. Under the first row of shingles we nailed a ¼-in. by 1½-in. strip along the bottom sill to tip the bottom out so it would look like the courses that followed. These shingles had predrilled holes at the top so you could fasten them to the wall with small nails. The second course lapped over the first by 1 in. and was nailed in place.

At that time we had no knowledge that working with this asbestos-laden material could be dangerous to our health. I must not have breathed in much, because 60-some years later I am still here. Probably what saved me was that, other than an old table-saw with no guard, we didn't have power tools. Cutting or drilling this material would have caused lots of dust. The material itself is stable, quite hard, and brittle. We cut it to length either by scoring it with a hardened knife or by cutting it with a device that operated a bit like a guillotine.

The roof, too, was sheathed with 1× stock and nailed to the rafters. Once the tarpaper was down, we began covering the roof with cedar shingles. It was here, armed with a shingling hatchet and a cloth apron full of small nails, that I was at last allowed to do some nailing. The hatchet part was used to split a shingle to width when you came to the edge of the building. The hammer part of the hatchet was used to drive the nails. I wasn't fast, but Adolph said my work looked good: the old master encouraging his helper.

Once the roof was shingled, Adolph and others began on the inside, installing plumbing pipes and electrical wire, plastering the interior walls, painting, laying the hardwood floor, setting cabinets, hanging doors, and doing the finish work. For me, it was back to school for my senior year.

AFTER ALL THESE YEARS OF LIVING ELSEWHERE, my home base, my specific place, my roots, the country where my heart is, is still western Nebraska. North of Harrison there is a long, rather narrow ridge of hills covered with Ponderosa pines stunted by the harsh climate. I spent many a day and night camping in this area, exploring all the streams, picking chokecherries, wild grapes, and plums, catching trout, watching raccoons as they watched me, naming birds, stalking deer, squirrels, and other small animals as they went about their varied lives. This is where I learned that the earth is sacred, complete, and the producer of all life.

What could be found along the top and bottom of the Pine Ridge was of special interest. Many, many rings of stones, along with fire pits that still held ashes were visible, locating the places where Native people placed their tepees. A Lakota elder told me that once the prairie sod inside their tepee became worn down, they simply moved it to another spot. This allowed Mother Nature to restore the earth. Are we modern, "civilized" people the only ones who do things to our homeland that nothing can restore?

I used to love to stand on hilltops envisioning where Crazy Horse stood in times past and take a long look in the clear air off toward the Black Hills in South Dakota 80 miles to the north and to the Rawhide Mountains in Wyoming to the west. Crazy Horse was killed at Fort Robinson, 20 miles farther east. I have stood in his death spot many times and let his energy fill my heart. Heady stuff for a growing boy.

The plains Indians were still free and active until the later part of the 1800s. Crazy Horse, an Oglala Lakota, was killed in 1877, a year after the Battle of the Little Bighorn with Custer and the 7th Cavalry. After that, their traditional life on these unfenced plains came to an end. Reservation life, with all its poverty, cultural desecration, and hardships, awaited the tribes. They were being civilized, after all. Part of this process was trying to live in wood-frame government houses that they hated. Old photos often show Native people living in a tepee in front of an unused house. Cultures do differ. Why should we not respect that? After all, "If you want me to be like you, who will be like me?"

I LEFT HOME IN MAY with a high school classmate, not even staying for my graduation ceremony. Many of us fled the dust bowl, the snow bowl, and the rust bowl to go south into the cities looking for jobs. I wasn't destined to be a small-time rancher, which was about the only job opportunity in our part of the world. Anyway, the small farms and ranches were disappearing into larger and larger landholdings, often owned by absentee landlords. The gap between the rich and the poor has been growing for generations. My friend and I ended up in St. Louis, where I saw a TV in a store window for the first time. It was 1949 and I was 18.

We found jobs outside of the city working with a crew laying down concrete for a major highway. We were working with a group

Yes, that's a church steeple behind Brother Joe and me standing on a snowdrift.

of about 20 men, all of whom were black. I'm not sure why they hired two white guys. Until that time, my association with black people was close to none. Other than Native Americans, I had little association with people of color. What I remember is that the crew treated us kindly. They helped us learn our jobs and taught us not to work too fast so we would still be standing at the end of a long eight-hour day. Laying concrete roadway is hard work. They shared with us their laughter, songs, and food I had never before tasted. I am grateful for those days with those men. I already knew how to work. They taught me that the color of our skin does not negate our common humanity.

We returned home to be with family during the Christmas holidays. In early January I was preparing to leave to be with brother Jim in Albuquerque when the "blizzard of '49" hit our world. This was one of the worst winter storms in the history of the plains states, which is saying something for that frigid part of the world. Global warming, so people tell me, has changed all that. Winters now come later, leave earlier, and are not as severe.

Maybe one day soon, as the seasons warm the land early on, they will come with big tractors and huge plows to open up this virgin soil. Then they can plant their patented, genetically altered seeds, and rest in profit. I think this is known as progress, no?

For three days and nights, the blizzard raged; high winds piled snow, covering our houses and killing thousands of farm animals and a few people who were caught outside. Range cattle would drift with the wind, often going into draws where they would suffocate after being buried with snow. The temperatures were below zero. The warm air coming from the livestock would freeze a little more with each breath until their nostrils were blocked, causing them to fall over and die from lack of oxygen.

No car or train entered the town for 30 days. Mother was ready for this with her stockpile of preserved food, though she did send

During the blizzard of 1949, huge train engines with snow plows attached to the front tried to open the railroad into our isolated town.

me to the small grocery store for a 50-lb. sack of flour so fresh bread would always be on our table. Highway and railroad snow plows tried to open roads into town. The railroad plows would get stuck in the drifts, giving some of us temporary work digging them out. These trenches through the snow were filled again and again by snow being blown across the ground. Folks called this a ground blizzard. This is the way I was accustomed to seeing snow coming at our world, parallel to the ground. I recall that the first time I saw snow falling straight down, on a windless day, was in Denver on the edge of the Rocky Mountains. We were on a field trip with my high school class. I stood in wonder at the beauty of the large flakes drifting slowly to the ground. Like small children, we ran around with mouths wide open trying to catch a flake or two.

Toward the end of January we were blessed with a warm wind coming from the southwest, as sometimes happened in the winter. This wind is called a Chinook, named after coastal Natives living in the Pacific Northwest. Today, people in Oregon call this wind the "Pineapple Express" because it comes on rapidly, bringing warm air and rain from the direction of Hawaii. Rapid and radical temperature changes can happen in a matter of minutes.

I have seen temperatures hovering around the 0°F mark surge to 60°F in an hour or less. These warm days were seen as a blessing by some, but Chinook winds can cause lots of damage. Mountains of snow were reduced to rushing water, overflowing gullies and streams, washing out bridges and roads, sending fish on their way downstream, flooding farmland, and even carrying away homesteads and other structures. Chinook winds often leave as fast as they come, dropping temperatures rapidly, freezing everything in sight. This is the world of nature that we constantly try to control. But then, why not? After all, have we not been given dominion over all?

It was around this time that I was introduced to a small book offering words that I have carried in my heart ever since, sometimes forgetting their importance: *The Little Prince* by Antoine de Saint-Exupery. "Here is my secret. It is very simple. It is only with the heart that one can see rightly; what is essential is invisible to the eye." Some of his writing I paraphrase and add to with apologies to the author: When meeting someone we never ask does he collect butterflies; does she like rainbows or the sweet smell of jasmine in the night air? No, we ask where do you live and what is your job. And then we think that we know him or her. Where, may I ask, would we be if we would only stop looking in our minds for answers that only the heart can see?

What a gift it is to really know another person or even another place with our hearts. It is then that we can begin to see the magic and beauty of a dandelion growing up through a crack in the sidewalk, a startling sunset, puffy white clouds in a blue sky, a drifting feather, or the weathered face of an old woman bent over by the years. We rush by such treasures seen only by the heart.

I close this chapter with a poem about, what else, the wind. It has been helpful to me on my journey. 🪶

The Wind, One Brilliant Day

The wind, one brilliant day, called
To my soul with an odor of jasmine.

"In return for the odor of my jasmine,
I'd like all the odor of your roses."

"I have no roses. All the flowers
In my garden are dead."

"Well then I'll take the withered petals
And the yellow leaves and the waters of the fountain."

The wind left. And I wept. And I said to myself,
"What have you done with the garden that was entrusted to you?"

—Antonio Machado, TRANSLATED BY ROBERT BLY

"We haven't accepted—we can't really believe—that the most characteristic product of our age of scientific miracles is junk, but that is so. And we still think and behave as though we face an unspoiled continent, with thousands of acres of living space for every man. We still sing 'America the Beautiful' as though we had not created in it, by strenuous effort, at great expense, and with dauntless self-praise, an unprecedented ugliness."

—Wendell Berry, *THE RISE*

CHAPTER SIX

The Adobe

OH, THE OCOTILLO. I didn't see it in bloom the first time I crossed the desert in 1950. It was there alright, in what I saw as a desolate, sun-baked, water-deprived, sandy world. My perception told me that these dry, slender, stick-looking plants were old and dead. I didn't have a clue what I was missing. As I have heard say, "We don't see things as they are. We see things as we are."

The ocotillo, one of the many hidden wonders of the desert, often grows 30 ft. tall, with tentacles like an octopus stretching toward the sky. Like all desert life, it has patience, sitting and waiting. And when the rains do come, which they do now and then, it is ready. Bang! It bursts forth with small green leaves along the entire length of each stalk. And at its very tippy top a cluster of reddish flowers blazes forth, nursed and pollinated by hummingbirds.

I had to be in the Southwest, the Great American Desert, for several years before I began to see and understand its beauty. Just

> **"I had to be in the Southwest, the Great American Desert, for several years before I began to see and understand its beauty."**

like passing through the Sand-hill country of Nebraska (or anywhere else for that matter), what is really there is often invisible to the eye.

Just as the ocotillo is natural to the Southwest, so is building with adobe. This building material has been used not only in this country for centuries but also throughout the world for thousands of years. Adobe bricks are easy to make, durable, and inexpensive if you do the work yourself. So as the quality of our lumber continues to deteriorate, we can once again turn to Mother Earth for our basic construction materials. Adobe seems to be a viable solution for many different buildings. The basic adobe material is underfoot, so there are no huge transportation charges. Bricks can be made with semi-skilled labor. Once the earth is mixed with water it is dried by solar energy. I think it's fair to say that it meets most every green-based ecological principle.

WHEN THE ROADS WERE FINALLY OPEN around Harrison after the blizzard of '49, I packed my bag and boarded "the dog," as people affectionately called the Greyhound® bus, our way out of town to the outside world. I was just another in a long line of country boys headed off to the city in search of work. And although I was quite prepared to meet this new world as a worker, I was quite unprepared in many other ways—socially, emotionally, and intellectually—but I had an open heart that wanted to learn.

My destination was Albuquerque, where my older brother Jim, safely back from Guam, had settled with his family and was working in the beginning-to-boom construction industry. They lived in a warm and welcoming home, my first encounter with an adobe house. I stayed in Albuquerque for only a few months that time, building tract homes, but would return 20 years later to actually help build an adobe house for some long-time friends.

Building with earth, as with the soddy and the dugout, allows me to roll out an overused word: *organic*. Adobe bricks come from the soil. Houses made from these bricks don't seem to intrude on the land. Rather, like the ocotillo, they sprout from the earth itself and even add to its inherent beauty, all curvaceous and inviting as they are. Building with earth, along with unmilled wood beams for lintels and rafters, allows houses to be shaped and formed beyond the normal square and straight up and down design. Adobe bricks can be used like paint on a palette to sculpt and make present ideas and longings that often lay bottled up deep in the recesses of our souls.

The ocotillo.

Allow me to say at this point that one problem we have in building in this traditional way is that we often run up against local building codes. I do realize that building codes, along with inspectors, are quite important. They protect a homeowner from builders who might want to take shortcuts that endanger the integrity of a house. They ensure that a house is built to minimum standards, with quality materials that won't catch fire or allow a building to disintegrate before its time. But, and this is important, they can and do stifle creativity and in some cases increase building costs well beyond the means of many would-be home builders.

I'm told that near one-half of the world's population, 3 billion people, live or work in buildings constructed of earth: adobe, rammed earth, cob, wattle and daub. Not every country has the rich forests that America does, but they all have earth. So people build with the materials at hand in shapes and forms that fit their lifestyles and conform to their landscapes.

The most well-known historical adobe structure in our country is the Taos Pueblo in northern New Mexico. For centuries, this multistoried structure has been occupied by Native people. The Pueblo people built their adobe structures, protective walls surrounding their homes, *kivas,* and churches throughout the Southwest and in the Four Corners area. Many of these buildings are still standing and being lived in today.

Houses built from adobe, Mother Earth, are home to billions of people across the globe. The Taos Pueblo in New Mexico has been occupied by Native people for many centuries.

Sadly, our own government wasn't satisfied that these Native peoples were civilized. Not far from where we were working was a large complex of buildings that looked like a "correctional institution," as many of our prisons are euphemistically called. Well, that is what it was—the Albuquerque Indian School, established in 1881 by our government and placed under the jurisdiction of the Bureau of Indian Affairs.

It was just one of the many such schools set up across this country to "correct" Native people and educate them into our civilized ways. Native children, mainly Pueblos, Navajos, and Hopi in this case, were taken from their grief-stricken families and held against their will. The children were forbidden to wear their native clothes, speak their own language, follow their cultural ways, or even go home for a visit in the summer. They were taught that their way of life was inferior to the white way. They were being "civilized" (I think we call this "brainwashing" today). Why is it that we need to believe that our way of living and being is better and more civilized than others? Which is better, to live close to and in balance with Mother Earth, knowing and honoring the cycles of life, or to race on asphalt strips in our automobiles to Las Vegas so we can spend money in slot machines? Just asking.

IT WAS HERE IN 1970 in the shadow of this old school that I was introduced to working with adobe in Coralles. Friends had asked me come to the Albuquerque area and help them build their own adobe home. Making adobe bricks has almost always been labor-intensive work: shovel the ingredients, stir the muddy mixture, and place it in forms one brick at a time. Nowadays, there are machines that can increase production from several hundred bricks a day to thousands. No need to invite all your friends over for a brick-making party, just buy a machine. I have a friend who built her own small adobe house by hand. It took her three years working on weekends to make enough bricks, but she did it. It is her cherished home that welcomes her daily with outstretched arms.

The basic mixture of an adobe brick is quite simple: clay, sand, straw, and emulsified asphalt, which keeps bricks from absorbing moisture. The asphalt can usually be eliminated if the exterior walls are plastered. Clay helps bind the earthy sand together, and

Thick walls made from adobe bricks offer a high degree of insulation from extreme cold and extreme heat, which means less use of energy resources.

straw acts to reinforce the brick—a little like a steel bar in concrete. My friend also added another common ingredient, manure from her goats. Once these bricks have partially sun-dried in their forms, they are stacked until completely dry and ready for use.

I have forgotten the name of the craftsman who taught me how to "lay up" adobe bricks with a mason's trowel and mud mixture. He was a master of his craft, having spent years building adobe homes. His nickname, given by fellow workers, was "old Leather-lip." This name was always said with respect, for he was not just an ordinary brick layer. He was an artist. He came by his nickname because he was the only person anyone had known who could drink piping hot coffee directly from his thermos bottle. I don't recommend you try this yourself.

Modern building codes usually require that a concrete foundation be poured on which to lay the adobe bricks. This foundation is reinforced with steel bars. Once the bricks are wall height, another concrete bond beam is poured on top to hold the structure together and support the roof. Additional rebar in the adobe walls themselves, both vertical and horizontal, is required when building in earthquake country.

Between these two bonding layers of concrete is where the magic of adobe houses can happen—massive, thick, round-edged walls that often lean in, crowned with a parapet that extends above ceiling height, deep window and door openings, beehive corner fireplaces, earthen benches growing out of the walls, niches carved in the walls to display art, and *vigas* (unmilled timbers or joists) that support the *latillas*. These latter, thinner poles or branches are often placed across the vigas diagonally to form an attractive

Leaving the *vigas* (beams) and *latillas* (branches) exposed makes for a rich, warm ceiling.

ceiling pattern. Together they establish a solid surface for a weathertight, slightly sloping roof. Add to this an enclosed patio and beautiful hand-crafted wooden doors and we begin to understand the beauty these houses can express.

All our work on the adobe house took place in the shadow of the Sandia Mountains to the south of the city and within rock-throwing distance of *El Rio Grande* that flows nearby. *Sandia* is the Spanish word for watermelon. Some say this name was given to the mountains because their sides cast a reddish-melon glow when the sun sets in the west. Wherever the name comes from, it is worth taking time to stop, breathe deeply, and watch the color display on the mountainsides as the sun slides below the horizon. This seems to be a fitting close to any day, no matter how stressful it may have been.

Deep within these mountains you can find hidden treasures dating back to prehistoric times. The Sandia Man Cave is one such place. Human tools and bones of extinct animals have been found there that are more than 10,000 years old. I spent some time in and around that cave, sitting quietly, fantasizing about the lives of these Stone Age people, imagining that mastodons and saber-toothed tigers were on the loose nearby.

Also stored deep within these mountains, I am told, are many nuclear weapons, ready in case we want to bring about the end of our world. Please help me understand this. Here we have prehistoric treasures sitting on top of weapons that can wipe out all history. Does this sound strange to you? Pardon my cynicism about weapons of mass destruction, but will these uncivilized, inhuman bombs keep our world "safe for democracy"?

The Rio Grande is truly a grand river. The Spanish conquistadores, who came in the 1500s looking for gold and souls to save, recorded their encounters with this waterway as several distinct rivers. It starts as a small mountain stream in the Colorado Rockies and flows almost 2,000 miles to the Gulf of Mexico. It was the lifeblood of the Native people who lived and loved alongside the river for centuries, raising their crops of beans, squash, and corn along with their children. Today, this second-longest river of the United States forms a long stretch of the border between our country and Mexico. Most of the water carried by this mighty river is used to irrigate millions of acres of agriculture land, so it no longer makes it to the Gulf. Where are we going as a nation anyway? What is important to us?

MY FRIENDS' ADOBE HOUSE was constructed with bricks that had been made in 2×4 forms. This means that the bricks were 3½ in. thick. Their width was about 12 in. and their length 16 in. This size, of course, can vary according to the desire of the brick maker. The thickness of the walls can also vary, depending mainly on wall height, individual preference, and the building code. I have been in churches with adobe walls 5 ft. thick or more, with huge buttresses on the outside to stabilize the structure. The walls on the home we were building were laid up two bricks wide, leaving a 24-in.-thick wall. The bricks were bonded together with a muddy mixture to which we added some cement to ensure a solid bond between the bricks, following the directions of the master craftsman. This wall formed a substantial thermal mass that is ideal for the southwestern climate. Daytime heat from the sun is stored in this mass and slowly released into the rooms as the night air cools off our world. Yes, the high desert can get quite cool at night even in the summertime. These thick, heat-collecting walls can mean low energy costs for an adobe home.

In days gone by, the roofs of adobe houses were sealed with a clay mixture on top of the latillas. With the advent of modern technology, they are "hot-mopped." One of the new smells I encountered in this growing city was the smell of melted tar, not the most pleasant smell on earth to my nose. The Pueblo style of roof is relatively flat, not pitched or sloped like a traditional gabled house. Roofers came with their tar pots, blackened machines operated by tar-splattered workers. These devices had a large pot to hold hunks of solid asphalt, which melts at about 200°F and is applied at about 400°F. Layers of felt roofing paper are laid down and sealed together with tar applied with a large mop dipped in a steaming hot tar bucket. This part can be dangerous, and care needs to be taken that you don't splatter the tar on yourself or another worker and cause a burn on an exposed part of your body.

The sky above the flat-topped mesa not far from the city is punctuated by five ancient volcanoes that erupted thousands of years ago. As the Rio Grande slowly cut through the volcanic basalt, huge black boulders were toppled, coming to rest below the

Glyphs, pecked in stone with stone at the Petroglyph National Monument. For centuries this has been a way for artists all over the world to express themselves.

mesa. This natural wonder was turned into a 17-mile art gallery by Native people. One Christmas day, I walked for 10 miles along this escarpment looking at petroglyph figures of plants, birds, animals, people, and other forms by the thousands. It was a reminder to me that our artistic souls need places of expression much more than we need bombs in mountains. Fortunately, a section of this rock art treasure was preserved for our children in 1990 in the Petroglyph National Monument.

It was also while wandering in this area that I had my first, but happily not my last, encounter with a roadrunner. It was watching me closely, not 4 ft. away, from its perch on a cactus plant. This desert-dwelling bird, a member of the cuckoo family, is an amazing desert species. For one thing, it can run at speeds up to 20 miles an hour. Little wonder Wile E. Coyote couldn't ever catch it. Maybe if we ate a diet of snakes, lizards, rodents, tarantulas, scorpions, small birds, and the fruit of desert cacti, we could move like a roadrunner.

MY FAVORITE PART of an adobe house is the beehive or kiva fireplace, placed in a corner of a room and often accompanied by a bench made of adobe protruding from the wall. In the winter, temperatures can drop below freezing. A small fire built in a bedroom will heat the earthen mass that forms the actual fireplace and radiate heat throughout the night.

Desert dwellers know the value of water, which becomes ever scarcer as the population in the Southwest increases exponentially. The number of people living in this area has doubled and doubled again over and over in the last 60 years. Because of this, water in some areas, as the old saying goes, is becoming "scarcer than hen's teeth." (I don't know if you have ever looked directly in the mouth of a chicken, but they have no teeth. They don't chomp on food like "normal" beings. They just swallow it and let inner digestive processes do the rest.) Predictions are that water scarcity will become much worse as global warming progresses, glaciers melt, rivers dry up, and the level of aquifers drops lower and lower. Sounds like Armageddon to me.

Because of the water shortage, you will often see barrels placed under the downspouts of adobe houses, matched with front yards full of native, drought-resistant plants rather than water-guzzling lawns. This is a good example of passive water harvesting. Fewer than 10 in. of rain falls per year in this area, making every drop of water precious. You can collect massive amounts of water from this annual rainfall. A roof area of 1,000 sq. ft. (20 ft. by 50 ft., for example) will produce more than 600 gal. of water from just 1 in. of rain. Who knows, maybe the next wars will be fought over water rather than control of the oil reserves of the world. After all, we can't drink oil.

Working on my friends' home gave me the feeling that I, and my co-workers, were complete—whole—that we lacked nothing. How can I say this? I felt that what we were could not be taken away no matter what happened to us. I had nothing to prove and what I was doing seemed to be something that fit into the scheme of nature. It was here in New Mexico that I saw a bumper sticker that helped to explain what I was feeling. One sticker announced that the driver had been "Born Again." Another, on the back of an old battered pickup, said that he or she was "Born OK the First Time." That's how I felt.

Much of my education has come from bumper stickers, and I am grateful for that. These days they are not so common. I guess people are too busy with their cell phones, texting or twittering, to be wondering about what a bumper sticker on the car ahead says. But for me, how will I further my education?

By the way, when I looked for the adobe house that was my brother's home in 1950, it was not to be found. Along with some other beautiful adobe homes, it had been bulldozed to make way for a new freeway. More progress, so I'm told.

THERE IS A COUSIN to the adobe house that deserves mention. The cob house, like the adobe, is undergoing a revival, especially in the Northwest. This is mainly due to some incredible teachers at the Cob Cottage School in Oregon, close to where we live. I spent a week there learning a little about building with cob. If you have a piece of land and friends with bare feet willing to help out, cob houses can be built with cooperative joy, lots of effort, and little money.

Cob building material is, as we say, eco-friendly, doing little or no harm to our environment. It too is a mixture of clay, sand, straw, and water. Cob is not set out to dry like adobe bricks, but placed in a wall while still wet and malleable. The traditional way to mix cob is with your feet. You can place the ingredients on a tarp, gather some friends, and play in the mud like children, letting the mixture squeeze up between your toes.

When building a cob house, or any house for that matter, it's always important to make sure you have good drainage and a solid foundation. Cob cottage people often use "urbanite"—broken concrete from city streets, old sidewalks, foundations, or retaining walls—which is laid in a trench as the base for the cob building rather than being carted to a landfill. Then the fun part begins, allowing our artistic side free reign to think beyond a fixed mind. All around us everywhere, the houses we live in and know have square forms, straight walls, and vertical sides. Cob invites us to shape and sculpt a house in various rounded contours as it rises up out of the earth.

We can be children again as we do the "cob dance," mixing mud and letting it squish up between our toes.

> **"The cob house, like the adobe, is undergoing a revival, especially in the Northwest."**

I found working with cob, unlike some jobs, to be a fulfilling experience. As a life-long worker, I have learned that often what we get from our work, no matter the kind, is a sore back and a stressed mind. If fulfillment comes with that, so much the better. There are many of us caught in work scenarios that are just not what we want to be doing, adding to our general unhappiness. Doing what we love is seldom called work, and happiness abides.

I know it is not always possible to do what our hearts tell us to do. We have families to support, children to feed and clothe, mortgages to pay, and all. It does seem reasonable, however, to ask if there are other ways to go about our lives. I know people who have downsized, live simply, and refuse to be caught up in our consumer culture. As a starter, taking a look at what we hold to be important might mean that we don't have to work day and night to support a lifestyle that is becoming increasingly unsustainable.

MOIST "LOAVES," cob material shaped like large burritos or softballs, are placed on the foundation and kneaded together to form a wide earthen wall. Gaps in the wall can be filled with cob mixture and smoothed to form an integral mass. Each level of a wall has to be built up rather slowly, allowing time for the mixture to dry. Otherwise the material can slump from the added weight. Walls can be built straight or shaped in whimsical ways according to individual desires, adding niches, alcoves, bookshelves, benches, and even sleeping platforms.

Electrical wires and outlets along with plumbing pipes can be installed directly in the walls, along with strategically placed "deadmen" that hold door and window frames, cabinets, and the

The beauty of a cob house shows up in its sculptured interior.

roof structure in place. These deadmen are pieces of wood buried in the cob that act as anchors.

Builders of a cob house like to use "round" wood to construct the roof. Actually this makes sense, if you are not counting your time. Working with natural forms and materials usually requires more labor hours than when you build with milled 2× lumber. Using round wood can be the ecologically sound thing to do. Builders use branches broken off by wet snow, trees that have been blown over by a high wind, others that have been killed by the bark beetle, or invasive trees that are crowding out the natives. The end result of these artistic, functional homes is a roof that can often stop you in your tracks when you see it.

THE COB STRUCTURE that I worked on had roof rafters made from branches of the stunningly beautiful madrone tree that grew on the property. Madrone trees grow in the mixed forests indigenous to the Northwest, but not in the plantations of present-day Oregon. I find this sad, because they really are remarkable trees, stretching their sun-tanned limbs upward in search of life-giving light.

We gave the building a wide overhang to protect the cob material from damage by rainwater. Building a structure like this from limbs does take time. It is much faster to cover a cob house, or any house for that matter, with a truss-built roof. But speed, at least for some, is not everything. Some people want more. A handcrafted roof is for those who deem that living in a home with such beauty overhead is what they need to lift their spirits and fill their hearts.

The cob house floor at the teach-in was a natural earthen floor. Other builders use bricks, flagstone, and even wood. The earth floor was put down in layers, hardened and protected by sealing it with several coats of linseed oil mixed with mineral spirits. The exterior walls were smoothed and then plastered with a lime-sand mixture. Lime is a good product to use on walls, as it will not soften when wet and yet it allows the walls to breathe. Added to this was an artistic horno, a cob oven, built on the outside, which produced some nostalgic bread smells and tastes for me. As you know, I am a sucker for real bread.

A number of cob home builders cap their homes with a living roof. The main difference between the living roofs of today and the soddy or dugout of yesterday is that the modern ones don't leak. This green type of roof is not limited to small, owner-built homes. The available technology allows large buildings, especially in Europe but even in our country, to have a roof covered with plants and even small trees.

There are many advantages to having a roof covered with earth and plants. For one, the roof is fireproof. The insulation it provides reduces the cost of cooling or heating a building. It decreases rain runoff into the storm drains. When a number of buildings in an urban area have living roofs it lowers the ambient temperature. The flowers and grasses that can grow in this environment attract many bees and beautiful butterflies. How can this be anything but good?

> **"The main difference between the living roofs of today and the soddy or dugout of yesterday is that the modern ones don't leak."**

Living roofs are heavy, so you may need the advice of an engineer to make sure the roof structure can support it. The waterproof membrane used by many is the same material used to line a swimming pool and, properly installed, should last for many years.

IT WAS IN THE DESERT that I continued my education about what nature has to offer. Have you ever thought about the diversity and shear multitude of plants and seeds in our world? I say "continued," because I first gained respect for seeds from my mother. Immigrants knew the value of these small, life-giving embryos with a living cell inside. As they trekked across the plains, they guarded their seeds like their own children, because, put simply, without them and their produce what would they eat? Each year, Mother used to let the strongest plants in her garden ripen, flower, and produce seed. These were harvested, packaged in folded newspaper, tied with a string, and placed deep in a sack of flour stored behind the stove to keep the germ cell from freezing as it awaited another warm springtime growing season.

One of her treasures was a rather large buckhorn seed that her own mother carried on their wagon trip west. Grandmother didn't

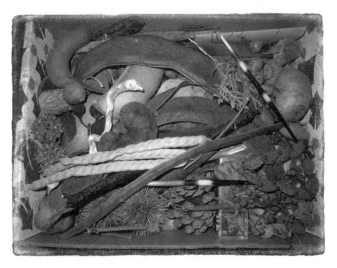

Do we ever realize that without seeds none of us would be here?

plant it on the plains, but kept it to help her remember her "home land." Before she died she passed it on to my mother along with its story. In like manner, I received it from my mother before she died. I kept it in a small pouch. Now and then, I would hold it and let old memories flood my heart. Recently I passed it on to one of my own children, gently reminding him, "It is not our seed that sustains the world. It is the seeds from trees, plants, and grasses that sustain us."

Maybe some botanist somewhere can tell us the number of different seeds in the world. I have experience with only a small, selected few, amazingly diverse seeds, mainly collected from gardens and public arboretums, that have come my way.

Seeds produced in what looks like a desolate desert are not only beyond what I imagine, but actually beyond my ability to imagine. We need look no further than the stately saguaro cactus with its bent arms stretching skyward. Every blossom produces around 2,000 black seeds, each about the size of a pin head. Over its lifetime, this cactus will produce millions of seeds. Their night-blooming flowers are pollinated by bats, doves, and bees. When ripe, the seeds are blown around by the wind, providing food for the creepers and crawlers that inhabit this dry, sandy world. Now and then one seed will find the right conditions, germinate, and produce a small plant that will grow into a giant saguaro. These cacti can grow to be over 50 ft. tall, weigh much more than 2,000 lb., and live 150 years or more. The next time you stand before this icon, you might think about bowing in respect. But be a bit careful about giving it a hug unless you are wearing a suit of armor.

Add to all this the seeds from the creosote bush, prickly pear, barrel and organ pipe cactus, the Palo Verde, yucca, smoke tree (yes, there are trees that look like smoke), brittle bush, the long-living ironwood tree, Joshua tree, jumping cholla, cat's claw, chaparral, purple sage, and vast fields of yellow poppies and we begin to see that we have a lot to learn.

So maybe the next time we eat something as simple as a carrot it would be helpful to our world, and to us, to remember how this veggie began. Carrots do not arrive at the supermarket "whole cloth." They, like us, have a history. 🌿

"'What is real?' asked the Rabbit
one day . . . 'Real isn't how you are
made,' said the Skin Horse. 'It's a
thing that happens to you.'"
—Margery Williams, *THE VELVETEEN RABBIT*

CHAPTER SEVEN

The Manufactured House

LOTS HAPPENED TO ME as I left New Mexico on Route 66 headed for the "promised land" of California in June 1950. It was a long trip across the desert that only a young person who thought all was possible should take. I made the 1,000-mile trip in a little less than 3 days, stopping to sleep in my pickup now and then. I was driving a wreck, a flatbed 1936 International pickup that I bought for $100 and that was worth less than $10. The engine had little compression and burned about as much oil as gasoline.

More recently, I've fantasized about making this same trip in a small manufactured mobile home, being able to stop when and where I wished. A home away from home that you can pull behind a car has a strong appeal for us nomadic people. Such a luxury could happen only in an affluent country like ours. A good number of the people who inhabit our planet don't have a primary home, let alone a second one on wheels.

The brakes of my old, battered pickup went out in Gallup, New Mexico, a several-mile-long tourist town spread out on both sides of the highway. I had an accident, hitting the back end of a car stopped at the one traffic light. The family in the car must have seen the look in my eyes and felt sorry for me. I gave them $20 and they sent me on my way with a "good luck." Thanks. I needed all the luck I could find.

I passed through the beautiful, still fairly pristine, undiscovered town of Sedona, Arizona, vortexes and all, and up the shockingly present, red-rocked Oak Creek Canyon to Flagstaff. What a spectacular canyon! How to say what I felt when I stopped to take it all in? An old song comes to mind: "Throw your lovin' arms around me." Yes, the canyon did that to me with a hug that lasts to this day. The road to Flagstaff is an uphill drive with a 3,000-ft. gain in elevation in less than 30 miles. The fact that I made it to the top left me believing in miracles.

The temperature in Blythe on the California border was 109°F when I pulled in at 8:00 p.m. in the evening. At least there was no snow, for which I was grateful. I carried a 10-gal. cream can with extra water for the radiator and several quarts of oil for the engine, so I made it across

There are many special, uplifting, even healing places on our planet that should be kept as they are. Who can deny that Oak Creek Canyon is one of those places?

the vast Mojave-Sonora Desert, looking like I came straight out of the dust bowl. I stopped only once, at a small, hungry-looking village that had a huge billboard urging travelers to come in and see their "50 foot python." I bought gas and felt no disappointment that the snake was a come-on. My mother had long ago told me to stay away from snakes of all kinds.

I struggled to cross the 4,200-ft. Cajon Pass between the San Bernardino and San Gabriel mountains. From then on it was all downhill to Los Angeles, the palm trees, the wide streets, and the cool, moist air coming from the endless Pacific Ocean that was bigger than any sight I had ever seen. Where I grew up we had a few streams in the canyons and earthen dams on the prairie with muddy water where livestock drank. There wasn't even a place to learn how to swim. What was I supposed to do with an ocean that stretched from here to Asia?

This teardrop trailer was my first home in Los Angeles. At least it was big enough for me to stretch out full length at night.

It didn't take me long to find a place to live, a teardrop trailer house in an affluent area not far from UCLA. The owner agreed to rent this manufactured mobile home to me for $15 per month if I would water the plants, flowers, and fruit trees on his property. The trailer house was small, with little more than a kitchen and a place to sleep. I had to go outside to a shower room that had an inside flush toilet with real toilet paper. Things were definitely looking up!

My little trailer house was not my first encounter with a mobile home. It was common to see them parked around the plains and on hillsides in Nebraska and Wyoming, dwelling places for nomadic sheep owners and herders. These "sheep wagons," America's first travel trailers, pulled by a team of horses and later by a pickup truck, were a smaller version of the covered wagons used by immigrants traveling across this country. They were compact, making ingenious use of the small space available. I have looked inside one to see a built-in bunk bed and table, a small cast-iron stove, a kerosene lamp, and a place for a 30-30 caliber coyote-killing rifle. Dishwashing and toilet needs often took place outside. Thousands of these homes on wheels were manufactured over a 50-year span starting in the late 1800s.

I became friends with a sheepherder, Raul was his name, and his faithful dog companion one summer in western Nebraska. His flock of sheep was not far from where I was working as a teenager. The English he spoke was limited, given that Raul had emigrated from his Basque homeland with little chance to practice this new language. He always appreciated my visits, which broke up his aloneness. I enjoyed

The sheep wagon was a common sight on the high plains, home for the herder and his dog. Must have been pretty lonely at times.

listening as he told sto-
ries from his far-away
homeland. One story was
about what to do when
the summer heat sets in.

"I enrolled at UCLA as a geology student because I knew a lot about the earth and loved the land. In reality, I didn't have a clue about what I was doing."

Most of us strip down to the few necessities we need to keep us
from being what some people say is indecent. No, he told me, best
to put on more clothes and drink a lot of water. Perspiration would
then dampen the clothes, and the wind would cause the moisture
to evaporate and cool the body. Something to think about as we
walk around in short shorts exposing ourselves to direct sunlight.
Maybe we are trying to look hot rather than trying to stay cool.

IN LOS ANGELES I found a job helping to frame a house the
old way. By this I mean cutting wood to length with handsaws and
building one wall at a time, nailing it together with a 16-oz. hammer. Production framing was still in the future. I was being paid
around $1.00 per hour, which was plenty to support my simple life-
style. Two days' work meant $16 earned, which paid for my monthly
rent. Food was relatively inexpensive, so I was able to put money
away for college.

There was a time when the education of our children was more
important than paying for wars. For years, tuition at the community colleges in California was free. The tuition for me, an out-of-
state student, at the university was $150 for a semester.

I enrolled at UCLA as a geology student because I knew a lot
about the earth and loved the land. In reality, I didn't have a clue
about what I was doing. They accepted me because my transcripts
listed straight As and I didn't have to take the SAT test, which
would have shown my educational deficiencies. I could read, but
my writing ability was poor. I recall sitting in classes hearing un-

known words coming from the professor. I knew how to talk about cows, horses, and the weather, but not about concepts, theories, and statistics. In an American history class I was given an assignment to write a thesis on the difference between Jeffersonian and Jacksonian democracy. I had no idea what the word thesis meant let alone how to write one, and could not recall ever hearing about Jefferson or Jackson let alone what they felt about democracy.

My little home was not far from Westwood, which is one of the most affluent sections in all of Los Angeles. It was here that I did my shopping, mainly at thrift stores and in their donation drop boxes, which were about the size of a large refrigerator. I have to admit to a bit of thievery, looking inside the boxes and choosing items without paying for them. For the year or so that I lived there, I was decked out in some cool threads. Even at work, I would sometimes arrive wearing pinstriped pants and a button-down collar shirt! Years later, I donated some money to Goodwill to clear my conscience.

These times, living in my little trailer until I had to go into the military, were lonely days for me. UCLA in those days had about 14,000 students, more people than I had ever seen before. Most of them, it seemed to me, came from backgrounds much different than mine and that I knew little about. They also were much more socially adept than I. I found it hard to fit into their world and be comfortable with their way of being. And how do you ask a young woman out for a date driving an old pickup that smelled like an oil refinery? Or invite her to my trailer home that had a ceiling so low that I couldn't walk around inside standing up straight?

WHEN WE TALK ABOUT manufactured homes, it can get confusing. "Manufactured" is often used as a generic term applied to many different types of living spaces, from the "home on wheels" you see on our highways, to prefabricated houses that can be delivered wholly or partially assembled, to trailer houses, and even to modular homes. What they all have in common is that, unlike a precut house, they were partially or totally put together in a factory.

Mobile homes as we know them today began to be manufactured around the mid-1920s on assembly lines, much like automobiles. Roads were improving and people were earning enough money to travel on camping trips with their "home away from home." Over the decades this type of dwelling has had many different forms, shapes, and uses. After World War II, mobile homes provided cheap housing for veterans and their families, allowing them to travel to wherever they could find a job. Trailer parks sprouted across the land like mushrooms. Travelers could pull into a park, pay a fee, and stay overnight or longer. In the county in Oregon where I now live there are many trailer parks where people live on a permanent basis. A number of these parks are "on the other side of the tracks," where some of the poorer people, often elderly, live.

Few of us realize how many Americans, often our elderly, live in trashed-out trailer parks—not by choice, but simply because they are poor.

And there are no hurricanes or tornadoes on the coast to clear out the riff-raff. I go into these parks now and then to build a wheelchair ramp for a disabled person. The state of Oregon has a program to help these poor people stay in their own "homes" rather than be sent to expensive assisted-living places. I never liked the sound of a convalescent home or an old folk's home, but a place that offers assistance in living sounds pretty good to me.

It seems to be part of our culture that everything needs to get bigger, wider, and longer. This is surely seen in the manufactured mobile-home industry, which has morphed from small teardrop trailers, to single-wide, to double-wide, to recreational vehicles out on the road that look bigger than the house I live in. Some of these RVs, so I am told, cost way more than a million dollars! My mind has trouble comprehending this. What am I missing here?

IN 1954, BROTHER JOE AND I went to St. Ignatius, Montana, to build a prefabricated modular home for our parents. They had decided to move there to be close to the Stockton family, Ed and Hester, our childhood friends the dugout dwellers. Remember them? Hester was born on the Flathead Indian reservation and wanted to return to be near her family. St. Ignatius lies in the Flathead Valley, between the Mission Range to the east and the Bitterroot Mountains to the west. Like Oak Creek Canyon, it is one of the most beautiful valleys I have ever known, full of waterfalls, trout streams, abundant wildlife, and endless spectacular mountain views. It is anchored by Glacier National Park to the north and by Yellowstone Park to the south. If you go there with an open heart, it will take your breath away.

The prefab house we put together (shown in the photo on p. 135) was a modular home used by the military at a base in Utah. After the war, they sold off many of these housing units.

My parents bought their building—a simple 1,000-sq.-ft. rectangular house with a gable roof and two bedrooms and a bath—for $1,000, $1 per square foot. Today it is not uncommon to pay $200 a square foot to have a new house built. At least this prefab house wasn't destroyed and hauled off to a landfill. It was delivered to the site by a trucking company. Wall sections, roof trusses, cabinets, and windows and doors, all crated, bundled, and ready to be set in place.

Modular, manufactured, or prefabricated homes all had a difficult time finding a market niche until around 1990. I remember speaking with a manufactured home–builder in the San Fernando Valley in California in 1970. He had built a block of 12 homes and told me that he couldn't compete with us tract home builders. Not only was the price of his homes higher, but in my opinion the quality was also lower because of the material used in their construction, which emitted a strong, "new home" smell. This smell, I learned later on, was from materials off-gassing toxic fumes, making people wonder why they felt sick. Often they were told by someone that "it is all in your head." Yeah, right!

I have a special fondness for the lilac flowers that are abundant in the springtime in the Montana valley where we worked. First of all, the flowers are beautiful with their soft colors: violet, light purple, lavender, pink, white, and even red. And the smell, especially on a clear morning when the sun comes over the mountains to warm our earth, really can make you stop and give thanks for being alive and present.

My parents purchased a plot of land on the outskirts of St. Ignatius that had a small stream running through the back corner. We spent our summer working on the house, cheered on by an audience of birds that gathered in the willows and trees close to the stream: wrens, warblers, chickadees, the outstanding western tanager, woodpeckers, crossbills, cowbirds, and the gutsy pine siskins. Our first step, an easy one, was to hire a driller to sink a well. The water table was high, so he had to go down only 25 ft. to find clean, good-tasting, unpolluted, and nontoxic water. He put down metal casing to keep the well from caving in, installed an electric water pump, and handed my parents a bill for $375.

The next step was more challenging. Hand-digging foundation footings for a modular home was quite different from digging into a Nebraska hillside for a dugout. When the northern glacial masses started retreating some 18,000 years ago, they forgot to take the rocks they had brought down from Canada back with them. This was especially evident when we dug the cellar. We hit one rock about the size of an automobile, forcing us to move the cellar to a different location.

Geologists tell us that we need to hurry if we wish to see the glaciers that give the national park on the Canadian border its name. We may have little more than ten years left, they say, before these huge masses of ice are no more. A friend of mine says, "So

The Andean mountains rise to more than 22,000 ft. They are covered with thousands of glaciers, many of which are rapidly receding, threatening the water supply to people living on the coast.

what, this is a cyclical event. Glaciers come and go." I am a backpacker who loves to hike the high country. I know from hiking the Andes in South America that the

> **"For a person standing on the edge of a cliff, a step backwards can be seen as progress."**

rapidly receding glaciers there are causing deep concern for millions of people who rely on water stored in the glaciers to supply their towns and cities. Places like Lima, Peru, with 8 million inhabitants, are "dry as a bone," having practically no annual rainfall. They rely on water from the Andes to meet their needs. Can we as a people do nothing but watch this impending disaster unfold? I like to remember an old saying in troubled times like this: "For a person standing on the edge of a cliff, a step backwards can be seen as progress." Do we have the courage to step back from what is causing all this, or should we just "damn the torpedoes and continue on full speed ahead"?

Our world and its people have some tough "water-wanting days" ahead, no matter whether global warming is cyclical or is caused by us humans, as scientific evidence says. My wife's family in the Philippines sees suffering on the other end of the scale. Rising sea levels now mean that some homes around where her relatives live are flooded every time they have a high tide. Millions and millions of citizens of the world who live close to the seashore will be uprooted if the melting continues.

As I look at the state of our world today, I'm compelled to ask if we have betrayed the trust between ourselves and the earth we walk on. There are holes not only in our atmosphere, but also in our forests, in our oceans, and in our lives. How will we live with our planet home from here on? Can we begin to have compassion not only for the abandoned dog we see roaming the streets but also for Planet Earth that sustains us and gives us life?

THE MODULAR, PREFAB HOME arrived by truck in remarkably good shape. This was, after all, a building that had been used to house people on a military base. It had evidentially not had much use, been deconstructed carefully, and shipped with care. We put down the bottom sill plate, bolted it to the foundation, and set the girders and pier posts to support the floor joists. We were short one 12 ft. 2×6 floor joist, which made us wonder where that joist went, seeing as how everything else was in place. (I'm guessing it was broken when they took the building apart.)

The walls for the house were made with 2×3 studs set 24 in. on center with some insulation between. They were delivered in sections, none longer that 12 ft., and went up rapidly. Within a day all the walls were standing, separating the floor into rooms. The outside walls were complete with interior and exterior coverings and electric wiring. The plumbing pipes were in the interior walls, which made sense: It does get freezing cold in Montana and pipes in the exterior walls, unless well insulated, will freeze and break.

Summertime in that beautiful valley may be as close to heaven as I will get. Having been around cities for a time, I had lost my connection with the moon, planets, and stars. We are, after all, the first generation in human history not to have a close association with the glories of the firmament. We can live our entire life knowing only the stars that come from Hollywood and not those in the Milky Way. Can anybody these days, other than astronomers and a few stargazers, identify even a little of what the night sky has to offer? I say a little, because I am told that our galaxy has 100 hundred billion stars or more. Amazing! What if they came out to brighten our sky only once a year? What would our reaction be then? Or does anyone care?

As a child, I was taught this rhyme:

"Star light, star bright, first star I see tonight./I wish I may, I wish I might, have the wish I wish tonight."

How precious those childhood wishes! Today we can't even see the stars, let alone make our secret wishes. One more thing that just makes me feel sad.

Maybe this is part of what some people call "the great forgetting" that has taken place in many of us. Do we remember our history, where we came from, our ancestors who came out of Africa, that there are stars overhead, that we were a slave-holding nation, what happened in Vietnam some 40 years ago, or that we are human beings who can have compassion for each other?

Many stars are in constellations that we can know and identify. I grew up being friends with a few of them: Cassiopeia, the lazy "w"; the Big and Little Dippers; the North Star, guiding early travelers; the Pleiades, called the seven little sisters; and Orion with his sword. They all welcomed me once again in that big, clear, smog-free Montana sky and made me feel alive and wanted.

THE ROOF STRUCTURE of my parents' new home was made from trusses that formed both the ceiling joists and the rafters. We set these upright, 16 in. on center, braced them well, and sheathed the roof with 1×6 boards. We purchased tar paper and composition shingles from a local supplier to weatherproof and seal the roof.

The roof was a simple gable so it was easy to shingle. I laid out the rows of shingles and my brother nailed them in place. Being up on the roof allowed us to stop and have a good look at the surrounding mountains. Often in our hurried lives we simply never slow down enough to just look. There is an old saying: "You can see a lot just by looking." Blinders on a workhorse help to keep its "nose to the grindstone." They also keep it from looking around and seeing the magical world that is happening everywhere all the time.

The worst part about the materials for the modular home that we received was the doors, along with their locks and the windows.

The doors and locking devices were of such low quality that we purchased new ones for the two exterior openings. The windows were single glazed, which offered little resistance to cold temperatures, as I realized from nearly freezing to death in the old frame house of my birth, praying then for any kind of warming, be it local or global. A local craftsman made storm windows that could be installed on the inside in the winter time.

I had learned some of the plastering trade from old Leather-lip while working in New Mexico. We decided that the exterior of the house, though not bad, would be much better suited to the Montana climate with a coat of stucco on the outside walls. This would reduce the possibility of pinholes in the walls that could let in huge amounts of cold air. We wrapped tar paper over the exterior siding and then nailed on chicken wire to bond the stucco securely to the walls. Brother Joe did the mixing in the old electric mixer and I, with hawk and trowel in hand, applied the traditional three coats of mud. A hawk, in case you have never seen one, is a flat piece of metal, about 16 in. square, with a handle in the center. The plaster mix is placed on this, scooped off with a trowel, and applied to the wall. There used to be thousands of people employed in this trade, victims of technology and "progress."

Methods and materials to plaster interior walls and stucco exterior surfaces have changed radically over the past 50 years. Compared to today, when stucco is forced through a hose and sprayed on a wall, applying plaster with a hawk and trowel is slow work. The old way was to put on three coats of mud by hand, allowing drying time between each coat to reduce cracks. The first application, about 3/8 in. thick, was called the brown coat. Next came the scratch coat, which was also about 3/8 in. thick. This coat was "scratched" with a comblike tool to leave the surface a bit rough. The final coat, 1/8 in. thick, was called the finish coat and frequently had a pigment in it to give the building a particular color.

The interior finishing of the house went fairly rapidly. We had to buy and install new light switches and outlets, give the walls a bright, shiny coat of paint, and ready the cabinets for use. We had a local company fill the attic and under-floor joists with energy-saving, itchy fiberglass insulation.

> "If you...ever lived in a country without libraries, you understand what they have meant to us."

There was no city sewer available, so we built a septic tank along with a drain field. In the local library, I found a diagram on how to build a septic system. It doesn't take much, other than hard work, to build your own that should last for many years. We dug a large hole, set forms for two tanks, and poured the concrete. We hooked the house plumbing up to this system. Waste goes into tank number one, where bacteria begin the decomposition. The contents flow into the second tank for further "cooking." The composted material then goes out into a long drain field that is made from gravel and perforated pipes.

Blessed are our local libraries! If you, before the advent of the Internet, ever lived in a country without libraries, you understand what they have meant to us. We had only a small library in the town where I was born, maybe 400 books, put together by the school superintendent. It was here as a child that I learned to read and dream about being a ship-boarding pirate on the high seas, a fearless mountain climber, or a heroic detective helping people in distress.

We scraped, cleaned, and sealed the fir floors with a coat of oil. Mother always loved linoleum with a bright flower pattern to brighten up her life a bit. So we bought enough of this material to cover the floors in the kitchen and bathroom. This was the "real McCoy," old-style linoleum and not a synthetic vinyl. Today, linoleum is making a comeback because it is seen as a product that is friendly to our environment. Unlike vinyl, it is made from renewable items like linseed oil (flax plant), powdered wood or cork, ground limestone, and resins, with a burlap or canvas backing.

One Sunday we took a home-building break and went to the falls for a picnic. What is it about a waterfall that is so fascinating to us? Maybe it is the power that water shows as it leaps off of a cliff. Maybe it is the rainbow colors refracted by the sun from the mist that surrounds the falling water. Maybe it's the sound they make that is often heard from a long distance away, when the rest of the world lies quiet, a rumbling that seems to shake the earth, especially when carrying spring rain runoff. The Mission Falls, Mission Range, and surrounding areas were named after the mission church, which is full of wonderful frescoes. It was built in the town of St. Ignatius by Native peoples (some say slave labor) and the Jesuits in the 1890s, with a million bricks molded and fired from local clay. The falls are not far from St. Ignatius, awaiting your enjoyment. Tread lightly, as they say, taking away only photos and leaving only your footprints.

I remember having my heart broken the day we went to the falls. A beautiful little girl, maybe 6 years old, was there with her parents. She was playing with a yellow butterfly by the side of the stream, calling to it, twirling round and round, jumping with true glee. Once it landed on her arm and a look of bliss came over her face. Then it happened. The butterfly flew too close to the spray from the falls, was hit, and was knocked into the water. She called for her parents to help. They held her while she put her head in her hands and wept, sobbing uncontrollably. Lots of sadness and sorrow in our world, no? Best we take our joys where we can find them.

Mission Falls, near St. Ignatius, Montana.

We finished the cellar, lining the out-side walls with tar paper to keep moisture at bay. We covered the ceiling with heavy, roughsawn 3-in. by 12-in. planks from a local mill. We waterproofed these ceiling planks with tar and layers of tar paper on the outside much like a dugout, backfilling all with dirt. Here is where we put the well-water holding tank to protect it from freezing winter temperatures. On the inside of the cellar we built shelves so Mother could store items that would give them food during the wintertime. Even though she now had a refrigerator, a cellar was as important to her as the rocking chair where she took a daily nap.

> **"The art of napping daily was one of the many gifts my mother gave to me."**

The art of napping daily was one of the many gifts my mother gave to me. It is an art, a real skill. She could sit in her rocking chair in the afternoon, close her eyes, and be asleep in a moment for 5 or 10 minutes. That is my practice also, awakening feeling fresh, restored, clear of mind, and ready to be open and cheerful for the rest of the day. This cannot be a waste of time!

I meant to return to that Flathead Valley one day, but it hasn't happened yet. My parents' stay there lasted less than two years. My heart stores a memory of a peaceful summer that it wants to revisit.

MY DEAR SISTER, LORETTA, is a migrant. I say this because I know and love her. She was married for years to a career army officer, raising children in many different states and countries. I swear, she can pack her household goods with army precision and be ready to move to a new place in hours. After her husband retired from the military, her on-the-move pattern continued. Every few years, or less, she gets restless and finds another place to live, sometimes only a few miles away.

One of her latest moves, in the year 2000, was into a manufactured home she had located on a small lot not far from the Pacific Ocean where we live in Oregon. I guess that the old saying "you get what you pay for" holds true with most of what we buy. These homes have come a long way from the mobile homes of the past, but quality is still lacking in some areas. If you are purchasing one of these homes, I suggest that you do your research well and buy from a manufacturer of quality homes. All of these transportable homes come under HUD (Housing and Urban Development) code regulations set by the federal government and under local codes in some states. This ensures that they meet minimum standards of good construction.

A manufactured home is one that is built entirely in a factory on an assembly line. Depending on the size, some new houses can be totally completed in three weeks or less. It is quite a sight to watch this process. The floor frame comes first, made from precut joists, lined with insulation, plumbing, electrical lines, and ductwork for heat and air conditioning. Everything is preplanned and premade. Workers know exactly where each piece goes, so there are few wasted movements on the production line.

The floor is sheathed with tongue-and-groove plywood, picked up, placed on a metal frame, and bolted in place. The vinyl floor for the bath and the kitchen are laid down and covered with protective paper. All walls are built in another area. Once complete, they are picked up and placed on the floor and secured in place. The completely assembled roof is then placed across the walls. Walls are covered and insulation is blown into the roof. The roof is then sheathed and shingled. Everything is painted, appliances and cabinets are placed in position, carpet is laid, and the doors are hung in the openings. A check is then run to see if everything works properly, and the building is ready to ship.

My sister's house was a double-wide and was brought to the job site in two sections by a tractor truck pulling a flatbed trailer.

These days it is a common sight to see a section of a double-wide manufactured home being transported from factory to building site.

Each section was 12 ft. wide and 50 ft. long, for a total of 1,200 sq. ft. The maximum size you can transport in Oregon is 70 ft. long and 15 ft. 6 in. wide. You often see these trucks on the highway with their flashing lights and "oversize load" signs. Her house was built in northern Oregon and hauled about 200 miles to her lot. Hauling any house that far over roads that can be rough in places may cause considerable damage. Put that on your checklist.

Her site was ready for the delivery. The truck carrying one half of the home backed onto her lot. Workers picked that section up with jacks and the truck pulled away. The same was done with the second half of the home. Next, workers poured concrete footings and placed cement blocks around the perimeter to form stem walls for the foundation. With this completed, the two house sections were lowered and attached securely to the stem walls before being joined together.

The remaining jobs were hooking up to city water and sewer services and connecting to the electric power grid. The gap at the

Placing a double-wide home on a lot can be a tight squeeze.

ridge where the two halves joined was sealed and covered with ridge shingles. On the inside, the drywall between the halves was taped, sealed with drywall compound, and then painted, leaving no sign of a joint. The last major task was to build a two-car garage that was attached to the house.

My frustration, and that of my sister, was that it took them several months to finish what they said would be a one-month project. Phone calls to the manufacturer for minor repairs went unanswered. Most of the interior hardware and fixtures were of low quality. I replaced the exterior door locks and added dead-bolts. The hot water heater went out shortly after the one-year warranty expired. Was this planned obsolescence? And to top it all off, the retailer who sold her the house went out of business shortly thereafter.

The problem of toxicity found in new houses is not limited to manufactured homes, this I know. As I have gotten older I am more sensitive to the off-gassing of chemicals found in the manufacture of wood products used in house construction, such as oriented strand board (OSB), plywood, and particleboard. Fumes from paint or a new carpet are the worst for me. Carpets can be loaded with VOCs (volatile organic compounds). I walked into my sister's house with its new carpet and had a headache in a matter of minutes. Open the windows, please, and let's air this place out. Maybe we need to go back to the natural dirt floors from my mother's days in the soddy. My sister lived in that house for almost six years before moving on. That may have been a record for her.

Reflecting back on the time I spent in that peaceful Montana valley with my parents and brother, it went well. We had no need to be worried about clock time. We were on no one's payroll. We often worked steadily from early morning until the sunlight started to fade away, stopping now and then to watch the birds and the small animals as they went about their lives, building nests, raising little ones, all the while keeping an eye on us.

I realize that those were the times when I began to understand what time is actually all about. We tend to think, so it seems, that the longer we live the more we will get from life. We do gain more in quantity, actual number of days lived, but quality of life is not measured in clock time, years full of duties, worries, jobs, possessions, joys, and so on. One minute, one given instant, can be worth a lifetime when we are fully present. We often stopped work so we could catch the iridescent glow from the feathers of long-billed hummingbirds as they sipped sweet nectar from red flowers. It is in such fleeting moments that "real" can happen (said the Skin Horse) and we can learn that we are not alone. 🦋

"I want to do with you what spring does
with the cherry trees."

—Pablo Neruda

CHAPTER EIGHT

The Quonset Hut

THE QUONSET HUT was born in one of our many wars. In many ways this hut is an icon of World War II, especially in the Pacific war theater. Yes, that's what they call it: a theater. The problem of housing the huge number of military personnel along with storing materials needed to wage a massive war was vast. Inventive minds quickly found a solution and started producing this rounded metal building near Quonset, Rhode Island, from whence comes its name.

There is a natural way of being that often seems to be unknown or simply ignored by us. But sometimes we get things right and build as nature does. Look at the seasons. Winter follows fall no matter what we do. No one can hold back these changes. The sun returns toward our northerly regions each year as the earth tilts in a new direction. We wait in nature's time, knowing that it is useless to plant our crops and gardens in the snow. Our moon wanes and waxes, affecting all of us along with the tides washing ashore in coastal regions. Who cares? We have our own agenda. What happens to us and to our world when we go against this natural rhythm?

I remember that one of my father's jobs was to teach farmers to plow and plant their crops with the contour curves of the land. To plow in a straight line is OK when the field is dead flat. In the hill country of the high plains, to go against the natural flow of the land meant that the little rainfall we got would run off and cause erosion of valuable topsoil that eventually came to rest in the Mississippi delta.

What does it cost us when we pay attention only to our hurried life full of things to do? What happens to our hearts and souls when we forget that our people have been following these ancient rhythms for many thousands of years? I find it good to recall that we didn't come into this world of ours, we came out of it. The earth, as it is said, doesn't belong to us. We belong to the earth. Pay attention to the land. Listen to it. Does "my way or the highway" work when we are dealing with Mother Nature?

We build our houses in straight and square lines. Where do we see this in nature? The Quonset hut is an exception. This strong, stable, half-round structure is shaped like a clam shell, the longhouse of the Iroquois people, or the curved home a turtle carries around on its back.

One common version of this adaptable hut was 20 ft. wide and 48 ft. long, 960 sq. ft., with an 8-ft. radius. This was followed by many variations and sizes to serve the demands of war from North Africa to the Aleutian Islands to the Philippines, but all maintained the rounded shape. My older brother, Jim, tells of the thousands of Quonset huts they built on Guam, a major staging area for the ongoing Pacific war.

The military Quonset hut was a prefab structure, fairly light-weight, compact to ship, and easy to erect even by unskilled workers. The floor was plywood placed on a steel-frame foundation. Interlocking steel ribs sat on the frame and formed the sides and roof. This frame was then covered with overlapping sheets of corrugated metal on the outside. It was insulated when used for housing and covered with sheets of manufactured Masonite® on the inside.

After the war, the military sold thousands of these buildings, some of which can still be seen across our country. People bought and turned them into housing for returning veterans, churches, schools, barns, airplane hangers, businesses, garages, and other facilities. Check it out when you drive around, especially in the countryside, and you can still see them here and there.

DOES ANYONE STILL REMEMBER the Korean War? Or is it just another forgotten war that happened elsewhere some 60 years ago? Even a casual reading of history shows that the list of our forgotten wars is long. I have to say though that this deadly war did have one unforeseen personal consequence: It opened me up, somewhat like a cherry blossom. I found myself far away from my boyhood roots, where I'd felt safe and protected. The war sent me into a world of ice and snow where anything could happen. I felt vulnerable, alone, but open to being painted with new growth.

The Korean War, which left at least 35,000 young, vital Americans dead, began in June 1950, when I was of prime draft age, and lasted until July 1953. At the time, I wanted to continue my studies at UCLA. I was also working and didn't want to go fight in any war anywhere. I admit to being shy of all wars. I remember what Gandhi once said: "I know many causes I would die for. I know none I would kill for." Some of us feel that way. I know the death and

> **"I sometimes wondered how I was supposed to tell the difference between a South Korean and a North Korean."**

destruction wars cause not only to our physical well being but also to our mental health.

And please, don't ask me about Vietnam. Nearly 60,000 beautiful Americans came home in body bags from that war; many of those who came back alive returned exhausted and are now homeless, wandering our streets, often mumbling to themselves. I know some of these people and my heart goes out to them.

The massive loss of lives, the laying waste to cities, the misuse of limited natural resources, and the financial costs that put a tax burden on all of us and our descendents for many years to come seems unsustainable to me. Will we survive as a people if we continue to kill each other as a way to settle our differences? Is there no other way to keep the peace? Are there no other patriotic ways to be an American than to join the military waiting to fight and even die in yet another war?

I knew I was going to be drafted. No student deferments were offered as they were later during the Vietnam War. Having seen what trench warfare had done to my own father and many others, I really didn't want to go.

As a young man, wondering what I should do with my one and precious life, I was encouraged by my elders to "follow my heart." Do what your heart tells you to do. That sounds like pretty good advice for all of us. Would not our world be a better place if we all followed what our hearts tell us to do? People with heart won't fight senseless wars, they won't strip-mine a beautiful mountain, commit genocide, pollute our land with toxic waste and chemical fertilizers, foul the air we breathe, poison all our water and then charge us more for bottled water than they do for gasoline, dump 4.9 million barrels of oil in our sensitive Gulf, pay their workers poor wages, destroy Native cultures, keep slaves, spend $35,000 a second on war (Google "cost of war"), rape other countries of their resources leaving people to survive on $1 a day or less, let the riches of our country benefit a chosen few, let our children wander our streets homeless, and believe this is what life is all about. Isn't it true that if we take time to look inside we can locate our real treasures? Are not the real treasures in us compassion, kindness, care, and love? Are not these who we really are? If we follow other than these, we do harm not only to others but also to ourselves.

Besides that, my mother reminded me that "war is not healthy for children and other human beings." Don't mess with your mother! A friend helped me to find a solution of sorts. I was a journeyman carpenter, so I joined a reserve unit of Navy Seabees, a construction battalion.

Boot camp at the naval base in San Diego, where young people are taught the "art of war" and to obey whatever command is given to them.

IT WASN'T LONG AFTER THAT, in October 1951, that I was called up for two years of active duty. I was sent to boot camp at the large naval base in San Diego and trained in the art of war. This means, of course, to learn how to kill other people, legally. This is what an army does. Let's keep the record straight, please.

I sometimes wondered how I was supposed to tell the difference between a South Korean and a North Korean. We were only supposed to kill those from the north. My wife is Asian, so I have learned to tell the difference between the Chinese, Japanese, Vietnamese, and others from the east. No they don't all look the same. But even with her help I still can't tell whether Koreans come from the south or the north part of their country. Maybe someone can help me with this.

From San Diego, I went to Port Hueneme, north of Los Angeles, for further training in construction. It was at this base that I encountered rows of the versatile Quonset hut set up for hundreds of different uses. I lived there in a hut for three months. This base is a training and staging area for military construction workers being prepared to build and fight in a war zone. I was there with a battalion of young men, more than 700 of us, all scheduled to be sent to Korea.

Part of our training was to learn how to build a Quonset hut, which was still being used by the military in Korea and elsewhere around the world on our hundreds of bases. We assembled one on the base on a concrete slab, not on the metal truss joists that were commonly used to support the plywood floor. A concrete floor makes a Quonset hut more permanent.

Before we filled the forms with concrete, we positioned a number of steel anchors around the perimeter. Once the concrete had cured a few days, we bolted the steel ribs to these anchors. The ribs themselves came in sections that bolted to each other to complete the semicircular walls and roof. They reminded me of the natural sandstone arches that you can see in Utah. Once the ribs were in place, we sealed off the building with sheets of corrugated metal. Each sheet overlapped the previous one to make the hut waterproof. They were attached to the metal ribs with screws that had a rubberized washer to keep water from entering.

Both ends were closed in with 2×4 stud walls and then sheathed with plywood. This gave us room for two window openings for ventilation and an entry door. On the inside, we used insulation mats that fit neatly between the metal ribs. Without insulation, on a hot California day the inside of a metal building can become "hotter than the hinges of hell." Over the insulation, to give the interior a finished look, we fastened sheets of Masonite to the underside of the ribs.

Maybe someone can help me understand what came next. It happened near the end of our training. We were preparing our gear to ship out to the Korean Peninsula when I was approached by an officer I had never seen and did not know. He came up to me with one question: "Do you want to go to Korea?" I answered—well, no, not really. He turned and left. I and one other recruit, from Indiana, received orders to report to the Seabee base in Quonset Point, Rhode Island. Everyone else was headed for the war zone. I'm serious, what was going on here?

QUONSET POINT IS THE HOME of the Quonset hut. There I was placed in another battalion and we were soon on our way to Newfoundland, an island province off the coast of eastern Canada, to build landing strips and a new base post office in the town of Argentia. People had lived in this area for centuries, but they were removed to make way for the war machine. We were there for six months, living on a troop ship in the bay.

The local Canadian people left the docks in their fishing boats early every morning with single-stroke engines that made a distinctive sound that I can still remember. I found the people from this part of the world to be gentle, kind, and caring—devoted to their families. They earned their living from fishing, mainly for cod, in a huge area of the Atlantic called the Grand Banks that lay not far from their villages.

The Grand Banks area was probably richer in the number of actual fish living there than any other zone in all of our vast oceans.

We were laying asphalt for a taxi strip at an American base in Newfoundland (I am second from left). You can just make out a Quonset hut in the background.

Stories are told how you could see uncountable fish swimming in huge schools most everywhere you looked. The people of the area fished the Banks for hundreds of years with their small boats and simple nets, selling their catch, which was processed and shipped around the world. It was a sustainable life with a renewable product.

And then they came, huge fishing trawlers with long nets scooping up their catch by the hundreds of tons, destroying a people's life and livelihood. Some call it factory fishing; others call it greed. By 1990, the massive collection of fish in the Grand Banks, like fishing grounds throughout the world, like the old-growth forests and the salmon of the Northwest, was gone. Unbelievable, no? As many as 40,000 people were out of work in Newfoundland. Is this not truly, among the many, one of our biggest ecological disasters? The effects of this disaster may take centuries to repair. Some say the fish will never return as long as Mother Earth allows us humans to remain in control. Can we continue to act in this destructive way and expect to survive? In the words of Jonas Salk, "If all insects would disappear from the earth, all human life would end. If all human life vanished from the earth, all life forms would flourish."

What's wrong with this picture? Why do we do this to our natural resources? How can we act so destructively with that which sustains our lives? Where does this short-sighted greed come from? Is greed built into our DNA or is this corporate capitalism at its best destroying what nature gave to us all for the "almighty dollar"? Why do we act like there is no tomorrow to worry about? The old ones of my childhood told me to "always look beyond the end of my nose" before I acted. Just thinking about it brings another wave of sadness over me.

THE POST OFFICE we constructed on the base was a super-size Quonset hut with a radius of about 20 ft. The actual metal building was already in place. Our task was to close in the front with a stud wall and plywood. We built scaffolding that allowed us to reach the peak. It takes some time to fit the plywood tightly to the

The Quonset hut was used in hundreds of different ways, from housing to hospitals. Here we are, taking a break from creating a post office out of a larger version of the Quonset.

curvature of the building. To simplify the process, we laid out all the needed sheets of plywood on the concrete in front of the building. We knew the radius, so we were able to figure out where to hold one end of a string to mark the curve. On the other end of the line we held a pencil and scribed the radius on the plywood. This way we were able to mark the cutline on all the panels at once.

On the interior, I was able to use my framing skills to build the stud walls. We sectioned off areas for mail to be received, sorted, and delivered. Some of the high walls went clear to the ceiling. We were all fairly skilled construction workers, so it was like working on a civilian job while wearing military clothes.

THE SIX MONTHS in Newfoundland passed quickly and we returned to Rhode Island to prepare to go to Guantanamo Bay (yes, Gitmo) to do some construction there. Again it happened. Shortly before we were ready to leave for Cuba, another officer came to me. He said that there was a special group that had been undergoing survival training in Canada and were preparing to leave shortly for an experimental task on the Greenland icecap. The carpenter who was part of this small group had an appendectomy and wouldn't be going on this expedition. Would I be willing to take his place?

Maybe he asked me because my records showed that I came from western Nebraska, where winters can be almost as bad as those in Greenland. I said yes. The nine-member group I joined had three mechanics, an electrician, a cook, two equipment operators, an officer, and me the carpenter. It was called the U.S. Navy Seabee Hardtop Detachment, and we left for Greenland around Christmastime in 1952. Greenland is the world's largest island, about three times the size of Texas. The Greenlanders have home rule, but the island is still owned by Denmark and is mainly covered by a thick, now rapidly melting, ice sheet.

We arrived at Thule Air Force Base, located on the west coast of Greenland about halfway

> **"Looking out in all four directions and seeing nothing but whiteness is as close as I have ever come to an understanding, a feeling of infinity—or maybe it was just plain emptiness."**

between the Arctic Circle and the North Pole. This is the site of an extensive, and expensive, Air Force base that was heavily used during the long Cold War. The native Inuit who lived there were given days to move farther north from their ancestral home. The base was chosen because it is midway between New York and Russia. In case a war of mutual annihilation took place between the two, weapons of mass destruction were to be transported through Thule until both nations lay in ruin.

It was here, out on the icecap, that I made close friends with an adaptation of the standard Quonset hut, the Jamesway, designed for arctic weather conditions. Jamesway huts are great structures, easy to assemble, and quite warm when heated with a small stove. They are covered with insulated blankets rather than corrugated iron sheets; I wish we would have had them in western Nebraska in the 1930s.

Greenland, at least for now, is a misnomer. Global warming may very well "green up" this frozen land. But for those who take time to look and really see, even the frozen, ice-covered parts of our world have beauty. I often stood out on that sea of ice miles from anyone. It gave me the same feeling I had standing on the endless, short-grass prairie. The knowledge I gained wasn't anything intellectual. The mind, in my experience, can't grasp vastness, but the heart can. Looking out in all four directions and seeing nothing but whiteness is as close as I have ever come to an understanding, a feeling of infinity—or maybe it was just plain emptiness.

When we arrived at the base, we came in flying low over the ice sheet. We were able to look down into huge crevasses opened in massive glaciers as they approached the sea. The blue reflected up from those cracks in the ice has to be seen, as words to relate that color are not in my vocabulary—they were blue-blue. It was like the color of a mountain bluebird. With the breakup of the seas in the springtime, the deep-water port was home to icebergs shaped in various forms by Arctic winds that can sometimes reach 100 miles an hour. Mirages of towering ice walls could be seen in the distance. Shimmering flashes of the Northern Lights brightened the night sky from time to time.

We stayed at the airbase for a while, preparing to set up our camp about 30 miles out on the icecap. Our project was to see if the nine of us could use heavy equipment to build an airstrip on the ice that would support the landing of wheeled aircraft. We spent our time in a corner of one of the huge Air Force hangers preparing our equipment, making sure everything was operational, as they say in the military.

A C-47 ski plane brings supplies to our small base on the endless Greenland icecap.

All of our equipment, the two Jamesway huts, food, stoves, fuel, tools, heavy machines, clothing, bedding, and, yes, even toilet paper was transported up to our isolated station by a C-47 aircraft and unloaded by hand. The plane had been fitted with skis so it could land on the snow and ice. In February, when the light began to return to the northern skies, we left for our station. Until then it was dark day and night. I recall seeing the sun come over the horizon for the first time after the winter darkness. Sunrise 'til sunset lasted about five minutes, as the sun came, peeked, smiled, and left. I bowed to the east, a confirmed sun-worshipper, and gave thanks for the return of this life-giving star.

Before we left our station in June, the sun was full on in the sky 24/7. I found the constant sunlight more disorienting than constant darkness. It disrupted my sleep pattern. Normally bed time is around the time it gets dark. If it never gets dark, how can we know when to sleep? My habitual pattern was broken and my internal clock didn't like it.

Four of us were transported out to our station on the ice cap. Besides us, the plane carried basic supplies, two tents, small stoves, fuel, food, and bedding to begin camp setup. We landed, looked around, unloaded our gear, and began to set up our tents. We cut blocks of ice-snow to form a wind barricade and a place for our toilet, had some food, and crawled into our sleeping bags. During our sleep time, a wind came up, tipped over the chimney of our small diesel burning stove, and started a fire in our tent. Scary, but no one was injured. The remaining five members of our small detachment arrived by plane two days later with one of the Jamesway huts, a larger stove, fuel, and other material.

The Jamesway hut comes packaged in the plywood floor sections, one section on top and another on the bottom forming a box. Inside the boxes were all the parts necessary to build the structure. We knew from the beginning that you can't build directly on

Our first shelter, a tent, was pretty fragile for living where winds can top 70 mph.

snow or ice if the building will be heated. Heat from a stove will be transferred through the floor and slowly melt the ice, allowing the building to sink lower and lower.

What we were building was temporary housing for ourselves, so we came up with a temporary solution to the melting problem. The plane arrived with a number of 2×12s that were 20 ft. long. We used these as a foundation for our huts. The 2×s were long enough to extend beyond the 16-ft.-wide edges of the building. We rested the ends of the supporting "joists" on other 2×s laid perpendicular to them. Before we left a few months later, we had a sway in the middle of our huts, but little settling elsewhere.

The two Jamesway huts, each 16 ft. by 16 ft., came in 1,200-lb. packages. We opened the boxes and set them on the 2×12 foundations, bolting them together to make the floor. The ribs were made from wood and joined together to form an arch. Each arch was attached at each end to the floor by a bolt. Each arch was attached to the next one by a spacer that hooked the two together. Once we had all the arches in place, we began covering them with the insulated blankets that measured 4 ft. wide. These blankets attached to the ribs, to each other, and to the floor to keep them in place. The

ends of the hut were also covered with blankets that had a vent for air circulation and an entry door. We had practiced putting them together back at the airbase, so even though we were working in below 0°F weather, we had the first hut in place in less than three hours. When you are in the middle of Greenland, you don't have the luxury of building slow.

The clothing we were working in was bulky but warm. One of our projects was to test various types of cold-weather gear. We tried out shoes that were made of 1/2-in. felt and others from a rubberized fabric that didn't allow the shoe to breathe. They were warm, but in a few hours time your socks were so wet you could wring water from perspiration out of them. Some of our thermal gloves and clothing were made from a nylon fabric filled with down

We built a structure out of 2×12s for a shower room and toilet.

or synthetic materials. I kept wishing I would have had some of this clothing back in western Nebraska as a schoolboy. I still feel the chill when I think of how I suffered through our long, bitter western Nebraska winters.

In less than a week we had the two huts in place, along with stoves for heating, cooking, and melting ice to use as drinking water. Our two small stoves, burning diesel fuel, made me realize how little it takes to pollute our environment. Within a short time, the endless snow and ice around our living space was coated with black soot. It helped me to understand the impact a million gas-burning cars and hundreds of coal-fired plants generating electricity have on the quality of air we breathe in our cities and throughout our country. City folk must have lungs the color of the blackened snow.

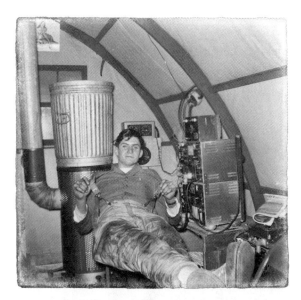

With no firewood within hundreds of miles, we heated our huts with a diesel-burning stove, and even in the coldest of weather, the inside of our insulated Jamesway was quite warm and cozy. The garbage can on the stove holds ice melting for drinking water.

We were not on the icecap very long before our huts were further insulated by drifting snow.

BETWEEN THE TWO HUTS, in a space about 8 ft. wide, we built a structure out of 2×12s and covered it with a canvas tarp so we could pass from sleeping quarters to dining area with ease. We dug a pit and built a two-hole toilet. Shades of western Nebraska! We set up a shower fed by a bucket of warm water, which was not enough to wash away our "sporty smell."

At the end of one hut, we built another small addition to house our two diesel-powered electric generators, one of which was always running so we would have lights inside. Once more, we built a 2×12 foundation under the generators. For the floor we used wood pallets that came loaded with our goods. This structure, too, we covered with a heavy canvas tarp. Before we left our station a few months later, there was a 5-ft.-deep pit under the floor where the heat from the generators had melted the ice. Without the 2×12 foundation, our generators would have been buried.

Rounded buildings work much better in this cold, windy climate than those with a flat side like a regular house. The wind blows up and over their tops. Once all our buildings were complete we were quite warm and cozy, and it wasn't long before our home was further insulated by snow and ice particles that drifted over the huts.

The Greenland ice cap is massive and stores much of the world's freshwater. The ice sheet where we were stationed was 10,000 ft. thick. Today it is melting at an ever-faster rate, to the deep concern of people living there and throughout our world. The northern part of the island is pretty much a white desert, so the melting snow is not being replaced. I read that if all the ice melts, a dire possibility, the water levels of the oceans will rise around 23 ft. Build an ark, prepare your lifeboat, put on your high-water boots, or move inland if you are one of the millions who live along a sea coast.

We also set up a large tent to use as a mechanic shop. All of our equipment—two small caterpillars, a grader to level the landing strip, a machine to pulverize the ice into smaller particles, and a compactor—came partially disassembled. This made it possible to unload even the heavy equipment manually by using pry bars and a hand-operated come-along winch. Once we got the material to the aircraft door, we slid it down a homemade 2×12 ramp. "Necessity is the mother of invention."

The large tent was used to protect ourselves from the wind as we put everything together ready for use. And here's a tip: If ever you are working in bitter cold, never take that last turn on a bolt to tighten it. We learned the hard way that frozen, brittle bolts, even large ones, would break. Out on the ice cap, we had no corner hardware store nearby where we could find a replacement.

We staked out an airstrip less than a mile away and began work. We organized ourselves, working 4 hours on and 4 hours off, keeping at the airstrip-building task 24 hours a day, 7 days a week. We seldom shut the engines off on our two small caterpillars. We used the cats to pull an ice-pulverizing machine up and down the landing strip, breaking the ice into smaller and smaller particles and then compacting it all with a heavy roller. Hard work, but at least I wasn't expected to kill Koreans. For that I am forever grateful.

IN A SPAN OF THREE MONTHS, we only took one break. We had a military vehicle called a Weasel, which is like a covered jeep with wide tracks for traveling on snow. Several of us drove this toward the coast to see what we could see. There are not a lot of animals out on the ice, but we did see some, including an arctic hare and fox, both white as the snow in stark contrast to the black-feathered raven. Ravens are the coyotes of the north.

We built a cairn on top of an exposed Greenland mountain to mark the sacredness of this part of our small planet.

They survive no matter where they find themselves. Farther out on the ice cap we saw a lone polar bear loping along. Later in the day, an Eskimo passed by with his sled and dog team. We marked our trip by building a cairn on top of an exposed hilltop.

If you have ever been in a whiteout, you know that it can be quite scary. With snow particles in the air and sun reflecting off nothing but the whiteness, you lose all reference points. You can become disoriented 20 ft. from the front door of your house. All sense of direction, except up and down, is lost in the whiteness that surrounds you. This is alright if you know where you are, but out on the icecap with no visual landmarks (and no GPS) it can be fatal. I learned in those times that nothing is permanent and that my own life is a precious gift. Enjoy the moment. No one guarantees that it won't be our last.

During one stretch of time we had a whiteout that lasted more than three weeks. A pilot can't land a supply plane in such condi-

> **"I learned in those times that nothing is permanent and that my own life is a precious gift."**

tions because the surface can't be seen. It was like trying to land in a dense fog. The coldest temperature we experienced was -50°F with a wind blowing at 70 mph. Exposure of unprotected skin in these conditions means instant frostbite, white splotches on an uncovered face. Anyone wandering off in the wrong direction in such freezing temps and high winds won't take many steps.

We had instruments to test the depth and degree of hardness of the airstrip to see if it would support a wheel landing of a C-47. Once the desired hardness was reached, we radioed the pilot at Thule airbase to give it a try. He arrived in an unloaded plane and safely landed, took off, and landed again on wheels rather than skis without incident. I guess we, like our former president, could say, "Mission accomplished."

Before we left, we took time to build one more structure, an igloo. This was fun. We used a wood-cutting handsaw to carve out large blocks of snow-ice and slowly form them into a rounded structure. Several of us sat inside, closed off the entrance, and lit a candle. It wasn't long before water was dripping on the inside, melting from the ceiling of our icy house.

We loaded our personal gear, drove the Weasel off the icecap, returned to the base, and left most all our equipment behind. That left me with a sad feeling. Even back then, I wondered how long we could continue to waste our precious resources. There was a lot of money tied up in just what we left behind, paid for by taxpayer dollars that could have been spent on our children, schools, health care, libraries, and decent housing for all. What does the bumper sticker say? "It will be a great day when our schools get all the money they need and the air force has to hold a bake sale to buy a bomber." Amen to that.

WE ARRIVED AT DOVER Air Force Base in Delaware in what we termed a "green out." It had been months since we had seen a green tree or lawn. The color shock was as disorienting as a whiteout. Back in Rhode Island, an officer encouraged me to extend my enlistment and go on Operation Deepfreeze in the Antarctic. I was tempted, but ready to pursue my studies and work away from the military. Two months later, I was hitchhiking toward California and a building revolution the likes of which no one had ever seen before.

My time spent on the ice cap was beneficial. I learned a lot about myself, blooming like a cherry tree in the far north. We pushed ourselves to the limit working on the airstrip, which calls for more than physical strength. It calls for discipline and mental toughness, with little time to think about girls. I found what it was like to live in close quarters with a group of men with different personalities. We couldn't escape, so we had to learn to live with each other's ways of being. It was a happy time for me in lots of ways. They even baked a cake to celebrate my 22nd birthday. This reinforced my experience that happiness doesn't come from things, but from how we feel about ourselves inside and from our relationships with others.

The dangers that we met in that frozen part of the world helped me to see that we are part of nature, not its master. Life there was one of survival unencumbered by a truckload of things that clutter our lives and keep us from being who we really are. And who are we really? I remember what a woman told me once: "I am just an old woman trying to live simply and be loving toward myself and others." It really can be that simple.

All paths, in the end, lead to the same graveyard. Living in the far north taught me to follow a path that allowed me to wake up, be present, and in touch with my heart. Please tell me, what else is there in life? 🦋

"Not everything that is faced can be changed.
But nothing can be changed until it is faced."

—James Baldwin

CHAPTER NINE

The
Tract House

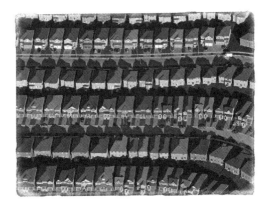

A CHALKLINE IS A TOOL somewhat like a fishing reel. It has a string in a closed box full of chalk that can be reeled in and out. Reeled out, it is loaded with colored chalk and used to mark lines on wood. Reeled in, the line is reloaded with chalk. The first chalkline I used when I came to California in 1950 was a cotton string wrapped around a stick. To load this line, I pulled it several times through a solid piece of blue-colored chalk shaped like half of a lemon. Full of chalk, it was held by one person on each end of the string and snapped to leave a line on the floor. Got the picture?

This tool, along with the traditional white carpenter's overalls, the 16-oz. curved-claw hammer, and the handsaw, typified why we needed radical changes in carpentry after World War II. The old ways were good for their time, but not for what was happening

You can see the evolution of a carpenter's aprons in this photo. By 1951, I'd given up the Sears bib overalls, like those worn by brother Jim (left), in favor of jeans and a cloth apron, which allowed more freedom of movement.

across our country postwar. With the end of the "Good War," thousands upon thousands of returning veterans, both men and women, with their GI bill and federal loans, needed places to live.

Between 1945 and 1950, nearly 250,000 new residents had moved into the San Fernando Valley across the Santa Monica Mountains from Los Angeles. By 1960, another 450,000 people would arrive. What they found was good weather, lots of jobs, and an unprecedented housing crisis. What we had to offer was 345 square miles of a nearly level valley floor on which to build. Along with this huge space and lots of manpower, we had years of stored-up energy and needs from the Depression and the Good War to help us get on with the job.

These days, I have mixed feelings about what was done to this prime agricultural land. The San Fernando Valley was filled with citrus, walnut, and olive groves, along with vegetable-growing areas that were incredibly productive. Large dairy cattle and chicken-raising land was part of the area, along with stable communities, often populated by Spanish-speaking people, who had been living there for centuries. A trolley system, the Red Car line with its 1,150 miles of track, allowed people to go from the valley into the surrounding cities and down to the beach when summer days got hot. There were still more people than automobiles, the air was clean, and you could see the stars.

As a housing-tract carpenter, I had little understanding of what the movers and shakers were doing. I did see things that troubled my heart, as when magnificent, centuries-old oak trees, with huge, shade-giving branches, were bulldozed into piles and cut up for firewood or hauled off to a landfill. Developers wanted clear, level land so they could build in rows and not be bothered by having to build around beauty. The dollar sign ruled. I had no idea that the valley would be crisscrossed by freeways four to six lanes wide each way that would replace the Red Car line and require that every household have at least two cars.

I think of the energy that could have been saved if we had oriented row after row after row of single-family houses toward the sun and not just toward the street and shaded them with native oak trees against the summer sun. Being used to the wide-open prairie where children could run and play, I always felt uncomfortable that every house was enclosed by a 6-ft.-high concrete block wall. My property! Don't trespass! With a little thought and better design, housing could have been built that reinforced being in a community and not isolated from our next-door neighbors.

For ten years in the 1970s when our children were little, I lived with three other families in a collective. We each had our own small home, but we shared many things in common. We looked after each other's children, taking them to their various activities, we helped with food shopping tasks, and we had to buy only one clothes washer and one dryer. Best of all, we ate the evening meal together, often sitting outside under a beautiful flowering mulberry tree, sharing the day, and watching our children play. This meant that each family had to cook only once every four days. Friendships and connections fostered in those times have carried on until today.

Change, even minor change, can be tough to face and doesn't come easy for most of us. We get used to our habitual ways of living, even when things are not what we would like; we prefer to stick with "the tried and true." Even a change like switching off a mindless TV program to read a good book is not easy. We get in a rut and find it difficult to get out.

But is not change really all there is? Is this not what all life is about? There is a story I heard about a man who kept a small fish in a bowl in the living room, feeding and caring for it. One day the bowl along with the water was cloudy and dirty so he decided to change it. He placed his little fish in a big bathtub full of water while he cleaned the small bowl. Once he was finished, he went to the tub to retrieve his fish. Lo and behold, he found his fish swimming in a small circle the size of its bowl in this big tub full of water.

THE CHANGE THAT HAD TO HAPPEN in the construction industry was not cosmetic and it wasn't easy for most everyone involved to accept it. Builders and carpenters had seen little change in methods, tools, and materials for 100 years. Houses were custom-built one at a time by a general contractor, who supplied both labor and materials and whose workers did everything from pouring the foundation, to building the entire house, to fabricating the cabinets, doing the finish work, installing the door locks, and handing the key to the new owner. A new house often took months or even a year to build from start to finish.

In 1953, my older brother, Jim, got a contractor's license. My younger brother, Joe, was home alive from the Korean War, so we decided to start a business. A carpenter's wage was around $2 an

hour, $16 a day. We found a devel-
oper in the valley who was willing
to let us do just the house framing
for a flat fee. We became piece
workers, being paid by work done

and not by the hour. Framing a small, 900-sq.-ft. two-bedroom,
one-bath house built on a concrete slab went for $90. A three-
bedroom, 1,100-sq.-ft. version went for $120. Framing included
setting door jambs and window frames, putting on some redwood
siding in the front, and making all ready for roofing and plaster. In
a short time, we were framing one of these houses complete every
day, making much more than our daily wage.

The fact that we were just labor contractors was resisted might-
ily by many older carpenters and by the carpenter's union, fearing
it would mean less work for its members and affect their paychecks.
I recall a union business agent visiting our job site in 1954. He
asked to see my long-handled, 22-oz. hammer. He walked to a saw
and cut several inches off the handle so that it would comply with
union rules. I went home that evening and put on an even longer
handle. Brother Jim was ordered to appear several times in front
of the union governing boards to justify what we were doing. There
is an old saying that lets you know how it all panned out: "You can
cut the flowers, but you can't hold back the spring." The revolution
in construction was on.

Given the size of the job to be done, we couldn't afford to build
one house at a time. We needed to find ways to build 500 houses
at once. Henry Ford had proved you could make Model Ts rapidly
on the production line. We were in the process of taking the production line to the home-building site. This required a change in
tools, materials, methods, and how we thought.

Many specialty tools that helped speed up the house-framing
process seemed to appear like magic. A bolt marker, for marking

bolt locations on the bottom sill plate, was a simple tool that made a time-consuming project easy. A layout used to mark wall stud location meant that you could leave your measuring tape in your pocket. Power tools just for cutting rafters for a roof simplified this task.

One of the biggest battles fought over new materials and methods was one that was waged for several years between "Big Plaster" and "Upstart Drywall." Huge billboards were seen all over Los Angeles telling people to "Knock on the wall. Demand genuine lath and plaster." Up until World War II and for many years after, most all houses in southern California were plastered inside. Good construction to say the least, but not sustainable in a production-oriented building world. Interior walls needed three separate coats of wet plaster, which sometimes took weeks to dry. Housing demands had no time for water-soaked houses that delayed setting cabinets, hanging doors, and installing trim. Drywall could be finished in days with minimal added moisture in the house. It took several years before Big Plaster went down, but down it went. Drywall had little time to rest in the winner's circle, as there was work to be done.

For us carpenters, the movement-restricting white-bib overall, sold by Sears, was the first to go. We put on our jeans and strapped on a cloth apron. Leather nail bags that hung on a wide belt with a loop to hold our hammer followed soon. The first of these

The carpenter's uniform became jeans, wide belt, leather nail bags, and suspenders to take some weight off the waist.

leather bags were made by a local cobbler in his shoe-repair shop. The large, open bags hung on the backside so you didn't have to straighten up to get another handful of nails when you were building walls flat on the floor. Later on we added wide suspenders to take some of the weight off the waist.

PRODUCTION FRAMING really isn't a matter of working harder and faster. It mainly has to do with saving a few minutes here and there by changing tools and methods. I worked with a carpenter from New York City who told us a story about his father, who helped build the Empire State Building in the early 1930s. Every time he had to make a measurement, he would take out his wooden ruler, unfold it, make the measurement, re-fold it, and then put it back in the little side pocket in his white overalls. For sure, it's a good way to make measurements and the building was built. We replaced the folding wooden ruler with a steel-bladed, retractable measuring tape that shaved a few minutes, adding up to hours off of every job. This is the essence of production framing.

The hammer that took the place of the short-handled 16-oz. with curved claws was usually a 20-oz. or 22-oz. long-handled model with straight claws, capable of driving a 16d nail with one lick. So was born the "California framing hammer." It began with the Plumb® rigging hatchet. This tool had a 28-oz. head, a grooved face, a long, flat 18-in. handle, and perfect balance. It was great for framing, but the hatchet-end was a little dangerous. So we cut off the hatchet blade with a hacksaw and welded on straight claws from an Estwing® hammer.

Before all the citrus and walnut groves in the valley were removed for housing, the Los Angeles River was allowed to flow free its full length on its way to the Pacific Ocean. On some streets in the valley there was no bridge to cross over. People simply drove through the water to get to the other side. I used to love walking along the banks and watch all the many species of birds, more than 200 different ones: great blue herons, snowy egrets, kingfishers with their long beaks, fly catchers, hummingbirds, wrens, cedar waxwings, warblers, swallows, and flashy redwing blackbirds, to name a few. Then someone decided that the river needed to be controlled, walled in with concrete sides and bottom. It became a fenced-off channel devoid of all wildlife. Think about it. Rivers have heart songs that they sing to us. To sit by a river and listen to its song in times of despair, depression, fear, loneliness, or confusion can restore our sanity. Why would anyone want to deprive us of this music? Tear down the walls! Give us back our river!

When I started out as a carpenter, I had a box full of sharp carpentry tools: chisels, drill bits, squares, hammers, and handsaws. The famed steel framing square with hundreds of uses was in every carpenter's toolbox for many generations. It was virtually eliminated overnight by the small, easy-to-carry Speed Square®. By 1951, I had bought my first power saw. It was a pretty dangerous-looking tool with an inadequate guard over the blade. Later that

Power tools like these circular saws radically changed how we built houses. They are production tools.

same year, I bought a used worm-drive Skilsaw® 77 for $85. In time, this type of saw, which I still use today, became an extension of my arm. Boards that took minutes to cut with a handsaw now took seconds with this power circular saw. I was ready to build.

Carpenters have traditionally been taught to "measure twice, cut once" to ensure that material is cut to the proper length. I learned that frequently I didn't need to measure at all. It takes time to use a measuring tape. Often you can cut an exact length by "eyeballing" the length you need. A good example is when you are cutting 2×4 or 2×6 wall plates, the horizontal parts of a wall, to length on a floor. The chalklines are all in place for plate location. All you have to do is lay the 2× plate in place and cut to the chalkline.

We also learned early on how to cut square without using a square. Framing a house is not precision finish work. Cuts don't have to be perfect, just close. So think of the time it takes to remove your tape from your nail bag, make a measurement on a 2× board, put your tape back in your nail bag, pull out a square and a pencil, make the square mark on the material, put the square and pencil back in your pocket, and then make the cut. To make a square cut without scribing a cutline across a 2×, for example, you can align the front edge of the saw base parallel to the front edge of the stock and make the cut.

There was a change in the materials we used, too. Plywood became more common for sheathing floors and roofs, replacing 1×6 boards. The 2×4 studs used in walls were precut to length, 92¼ in., at the mill. This with the three wall plates accommodated a sheet of 8-ft. drywall on the inside. Sizes and lengths of materials were standardized. A radial arm saw, commonly called a cutoff saw, could make multiple cuts at once. Metal window frames that were easy to install replaced the wood frames. Sheets of perforated gypsum board replaced individual pieces of narrow wood lath.

Concrete slabs became more common than full basements or stem-wall foundations. A slab poured one day was ready for carpenters to begin framing walls the next.

Not only did the carpentry trade change, all other trades changed as well. Actually, they had no choice. Plumbers set aside their smoking pots of melted lead along with their caulking tools and oakum used to unite iron pipe and began to work with pipes that were flexible and easy to join. Electricians too changed from rigid to flexible conduit and then to Romex® cables that could be installed in half the time. Sheet-metal workers put away their tools used to solder metal ducts together and picked up flexible ducts that didn't have to be wrapped with asbestos tape.

Over the years I worked with many different and interesting people. We may have been the only company at the time to hire women. They did well as carpenters, but suffered some from insensitive men. One of the guys I worked with for a time was a good carpenter, but he talked incessantly. I doubt that you can talk that much without being insensitive to most everyone sooner or later. One work partner told him he might best keep his mouth shut, at least now and then, lest he sunburn his tongue.

Still, the biggest changes came not in tools and materials, but in the methods we used to construct a house. This could have happened only because there were thousands of houses that needed to be built. People in the trades became specialists rather than generalists. The process of building a house was broken down into subspecialties. Roof cutting, stair building, floor sheathing, wall framing, door hanging, shingling, and many others aspects of house building were simplified and subcontracted out to piece workers. Piece workers were motivated not to work faster, but to work smarter and figure out better and easier ways to do their task.

Until the early 1960s, when handheld, air-operated nail guns became available, most all of our nailing was done by hand. We became master nailers, which is as much an art as a skill. Traditionally, the nails we used were ordinary, common nails delivered in 100-lb. wooden kegs. These nails came in various sizes and lengths, each one designated for different parts of the building process. Thick common nails are hard to drive with one lick of a hammer. Because we were wearing two nail bags, not the white overalls with many pockets, we began using two sizes, the 8d (d = penny = nail size) and the 16d box nail. The box nail is the same length as a common, a bit smaller in diameter, and easier to drive.

One innovation that sped up floor and roof nailing in the 1950s was the "invention" of the floor-nailing buggy. The buggy was a simple tool crafted from a piece of 16-in. by 16-in. 3/4-in. plywood to which four wheels were attached. The wheels were about 3 in. round so they wouldn't fall through cracks in the 1×6 subfloor. To one side of the buggy was attached a bread-baking pan, which held nails. This allowed a floor-nailing carpenter to sit on his bottom, rather than be on his knees, and push himself backward across a floor nailing the sheathing into the joists. There were people around, piece workers, who did nothing but hand-nail floors. They would take a 50-lb. box of nails home at night and wrap bundles of 30 nails, all heads up, with rubber bands. In the morning they would sit on their buggy, grab a handful of nails, take off the rubber band, and feed them out with their fingers one nail at a time. One tap with a hammer set the nail and one lick drove it home. Some of these carpenters could drive nails as fast as a worker with a nail gun.

One of the fastest nailers I worked with came from a sharecropper's family down in "South Georgia right near the Florida line." Born before the civil rights movement, he never had a chance to go to school and learn to read and write. When we switched jobs, I used to take him to the new site because he couldn't read the street signs to know where to go. But, please, believe me, he could nail!

Production framing is based on working more efficiently no matter the task. To make it easy to drive nails with one lick we treated them with a gas-wax process. We bought nails by the pallet load, hundreds of kegs or boxes. When they arrived at the shop, I took a 5-gal. bucket full of gasoline and set it in the sun. (This shows my lack of environmental awareness at the time.) Once the gas was warm, I dropped in a bar of paraffin. After the wax melted, I would open boxes of nails, pour in a cup of the gas wax, and shake the nails around in the container. The solution would cover the nails with a thin coat of wax and the gas would evaporate. Other people did the same with dishwashing soap.

These nails went into wood like a hot knife through butter. One lick with a long-handled hammer and a 16d was home. Building inspectors wondered whether gas-waxed nails had the holding power of a bright, unwaxed nail. I had to explain to them that most nails in a framed wall hold in shear and not in tension. Beyond that, once the nail is driven, the wax dries and gives the nail holding power much like a regular nail. The industry responded later with green sinkers, nails coated with a thin layer of toxic vinyl that drive easily. Not a good idea to hold these nails in your mouth.

I LEARNED THE HARD WAY that it is always a good idea to wear protective devices when working in frame construction. Good shoes to protect your feet, breathing masks (especially when the sawdust is fine or you are cutting treated wood or toxic materials), and guards on circular saws are some of the essential steps to take to keep you from harm. It really wasn't possible to wear gloves to protect yourself from getting slivers. Gloved hands can't easily handle nails. Slivers were part of our lives. The old-timers told us not to worry about slivers anyway—after a time, they said, "It was just wood going into wood."

I was working in the West Valley one day in 1954. It was hot so I removed my glasses, which were wet from sweat. Sometimes when you set a nail and then drive it you

"The old-timers told us not to worry about slivers anyway— after a time, they said, 'It was just wood going into wood.'"

will catch just a corner of the head and it will fly off into space. I was framing that day and a nail flew up and hit me in the eye point first. I thought it was just a bruise until my eyesight became blurry. I drove to the Burbank Hospital, and it wasn't long before I was in an operating room preparing to have stitches taken in a punctured eyeball. Ouch! The doctor who did the sewing was an immigrant from Hungary. I heard him tell the staff that he had 14 children. Thoughts about his poor wife ran through my head. Every time he leaned over to take a stitch in my eye I also learned that he had bad breath. I was grateful that he was a competent surgeon, but I should have gifted him with a toothbrush.

Once the operation was finished, they stitched my eyelid shut, bandaged both eyes, put me in a hospital bed, fed me a liquid diet, and told me not to move for ten days so my eye would heal properly. Try lying totally still for ten days sometime. My body became a mass of pain from inactivity. When my time was up, they removed the bandages and the stitches, re-stitched the lid shut, and put a bandage on my injured eye. Then they covered both eyes with a black mask with a dime-sized hole on one side that allowed me to see with my good eye. I drove home down a major thoroughfare looking like the Lone Ranger searching for Tonto. It took a couple of years before my sight stabilized. At night, street lights looked like giant amoeba spread out across the sky.

The movement of material—stacks of studs, joists, sheathing, and more—was a major task, especially on large jobs that had two or three stories. We simplified this first by using conveyor belts to move wood from one location to another. Then we started us-

"For the first and probably the last time in our nation's history, masses of ordinary workers could afford to buy and actually own homes; it was the American dream fulfilled."

ing fork lifts. These incredible machines can raise a stack of 500 2× studs up three stories and set them on the floor where they are needed. No more carrying armloads of material to a different location one step at a time.

Production framing is based on a few simple principles. The first is, don't sacrifice quality for quantity. I have heard people say, "We don't build them like we used to." That's true. After tearing down and remodeling many older buildings, my observation is that we build houses better than we used to. Frequently in old houses the foundations and footings were not adequate to carry the weight of the house, causing them to settle and sink. The floor and ceiling joists often spanned distances that were too great, resulting in bouncy floors and sagging ceilings. Door and window headers could be as simple as a 2×4 installed flat. Wall bracing was often non-existent. So what was lost in this massive building boom was not quality. What we left behind was all the handcrafted details that you see in a Victorian, Craftsman, or Bungalow house. These are beautiful but take time and money to create.

We were not building gingerbread houses, McMansions, or starter castles. We were building solid, one- and two-story tract houses that working-class families could afford to buy. Brother Jim, taking advantage of the GI Bill, was able to move into a new three-bedroom house in the Valley in 1951 for $400 down. With the median house price around $9,000, his monthly payment was $65, which included taxes and insurance. For the first and probably the last time in our nation's history, masses of ordinary workers could afford to buy and actually own homes; it was the American dream fulfilled. Nowadays, when many of us say "we own our home" what that means is that we have a 30-year mortgage with a loan company. If we miss even one monthly payment, we get charged late fees and face losing "our home" in foreclosure, "The American Nightmare!" Ambrose Bierce summed it up nicely with his definition: "Debt, n. An ingenious substitute for the chain and whip of the slave driver."

The first pneumatic nailer on our job sites in the early 1950s was a "walking nailer" supplied by Nu-Matic Nailer. It was a production tool, operated by a person standing upright while nailing off floors and low-pitched roofs. Four hundred or more regular 8d nails straight out of the box were put in a tray. These dropped down a tube one by one and were driven, rat-a-tat-tat. At the bottom of the tube was a loop through which you slipped your foot. This allowed you to walk along, driving nails through the floor sheathing into the joists. A good operator could easily nail off more than 7,000 sq. ft. of floor or low-pitched roof in a day.

With all the iPods and ear buds, does anyone sing on the job site these days? Many framers were also musicians, and they often sang songs to entertain us and make the workday pass. It was here that I remembered and sang songs from my childhood—"The Old Rugged Cross," "Just a Closer Walk with Thee," and Irish drinking ballads. Thanks much to the Methodist hymnal and my mother.

As a beginning carpenter, I made myself a wooden toolbox. Every carpenter carried one of these, a piece of fur-

CUTS NAILING COSTS UP TO 50%

USES CONVENIENT NAILS 6d TO 8d

SPEEDS PRODUCTION

The only automatic portable nailing machine with self-contained sorting device

NU-MATIC NAILER INC.

The walking nailer was our first air-operated nail gun. We used it extensively to nail floors and low-pitched roofs.

niture really. It held all my tools, a framing square, level, chisels, planes, screwdrivers, and many others. It just didn't fit into the new world of production framing, so I exchanged it for a 5-gal. bucket with a canvas insert to hold tools. This became the "toolbox" of choice for us framers.

Regular handheld nail guns that have essentially replaced the hammer became available in the early 1960s. The first air gun I had was actually one that drove staples that secured sheathing to floors and roofs. It wasn't until about 1962 that Paslode® came out with a usable 8d nail gun called the "gun nailer." Their 16d nail gun, "The Stallion," was cumbersome and jammed frequently. So we continued to nail walls together by hand until around 1970, when better 16d guns were available.

One change in our way of working that increased how rapidly we could build houses was a simple one. When I started framing houses in L.A., we would snap a chalkline for one wall, lay

The 5-gal. bucket became the "toolbox" of choice for most production framers.

down floor plates, cut studs, and build that wall upright, standing in place. Then we would snap a line for another wall, build that, and so on until all the walls were upright. We switched back and forth between tasks. The simple change was to complete all of whatever job we were doing before going on to the next one. So when we started building a house, we would lay out room dimensions and snap all the chalklines marking the location of every wall

In production framing, the job of laying down all the wall plates is finished before moving on to the next task.

on the floor. Then we would come back and lay down all of the plates, both top and bottom, on the lines before marking where the studs and door and window headers would be. This went on until every wall for every room was ready to frame. Framing was done flat on the floor rather than upright. These few, rather simple changes saved a huge amount of time.

WHAT WE DIDN'T REALIZE at the time was that some of what we were doing was harmful, both to our environment and to us. There were times when lots of useful materials left behind on a job site were carted off to a landfill. We could have been more careful about how we used lumber. We had no idea what was being done to the forests in the northwest that supplied us.

If you've ever stood quietly among the few remaining redwoods along the California coast and let them soak into your being, you might, like me, have been reduced to tears. There used to be many millions of acres of tall trees (and tall grass) in our country, but most of these national treasures are long gone. What do we value? What gives us life?

There is a lonely Douglas fir tree some 60 miles from where I live, the Doerner Fir. Now and then I pay a visit to this jewel, the biggest fir in our country. It is 329 ft. tall and 11½ ft. across. If you get the chance, please go there, pay your respects, bow in wonder, and give it a hug along with thanks that the timber barons missed it. What we get from a 450-year-old tree can make the heart flutter. It's a feeling a bit like the one we get when we fall in love. We find ourselves "all a-twitter." Yes, twittering was around before the tech age. How tweet is that?

I have seen developers tear down beautiful homes that were full of hand-crafted treasures so they could build a boxy apartment house with little or no space for people to gather or children to play. Toxic chemicals were being used. Plumbers working in a ditch gluing PVC pipes together would come out and stumble around dizzy for a few steps. They were unintentional glue sniffers. Solvents in paints, especially lacquer, asbestos in many products, formaldehyde in plywood, toxic glues in synthetic carpets, and foul-smelling vinyl products all added to what we worked with on a

Something happens to my heart when I encounter an old-growth tree like this one. I'm sorry, but I could never bring myself to dip my chainsaw into a grandmother tree like you see here.

daily basis. When this is dumped into a landfill will it ever disintegrate? We humans seem to be the only ones that can manufacture materials that nature can't digest.

The last time I drove on Highway 99 through the long, hugely productive farmland of the San Joaquin Valley in central California it reminded me of some job site smells. We stopped in a small town to buy gas. When I opened the car door, the air smelled like chemical fertilizer and toxic pesticide. Looking around, I saw nothing moving, no bees, flies, birds, or anything creeping or crawling. The people who do the farm work live in hot, dusty towns and not on the land as stewards. They are not even sharecroppers. What's up with this? Does this kind of farming give us the nutritious food we need? Is this type of farming done for people or for profit? And who is it that reaps all the profit? Do they eat from the same farm produce that we do? Just checking.

As a carpenter, I worked for years with 2× sill stock that had been treated with copper, chromate, and arsenic. Treated sills are the first piece of wood used when a framed wall sits on concrete. The toxic chemicals in the wood stop subterranean termites from eating up into the wall. For many years we received truckloads of treated lumber delivered from the supplier that was literally dripping with green, copper-colored liquid. I used to go home from work with my jeans soaked from carrying this material. I might as well have been drinking the stuff. In 2002 I came down with a serious case of deadly, incurable T-cell lymphoma: cancer of the lymphatic system. I am generally a healthy person with few aches or ills. Arsenic and copper have been known to be cancer-causing agents for many years. I had no idea these poisonous chemicals were penetrating my skin and entering my body. (I would have gladly protected myself from contact if I had known this.) In 2003, 50 years too late, the Environmental Protection Agency banned the use of arsenic in treated wood used in housing. Thanks a lot!

RAFTER CUTTING to build a roof seemed daunting to many people because of the way it was traditionally done. When I first began laying out and cutting rafters, we did it by stepping off the required measurements with a framing square on a rafter, laying out the plumb ridge cut, the bird's-mouth at the wall line, and another plumb cut for the tail overhang. Once the first rafter was ready it was cut with a handsaw and then used as a pattern to lay out the rest, one rafter at a time. A simple, common gable roof could take all day or longer to lay out and cut.

Several years later, I was cutting the same roofs in an hour or so. Rafters were bunched together on long sawhorses. The required length was taken from tables in a rafter book or a pocket calculator. Chalklines were snapped across the rafters, marking length and bird's-mouth location. The ridge and tail plumb cut was made across all the rafters with a large circular-saw blade. The bird's-mouth or seat cut was made by a saw with a router head or with a swing table mounted on a Skilsaw.

We were able to lay our saws over to more than 45 degrees simply by putting on a different table. This allowed us to cut the bird's mouths of multiple common rafters all at once.

These method changes were repeated for every aspect of the house-framing process. The end product was a house framed rapidly without a reduction of quality. Workers were receiving a decent wage, so those of us who were building houses could actually afford to buy what we were building. People even had time to sit in their chairs on the porches and decks we built around the houses, enjoying the evening as it cooled. Who sits on a porch just resting or chatting with their neighbor nowadays? We now go from air-conditioned house to air-conditioned car to air-conditioned office. Something about this doesn't seem quite right to me.

WHAT I HAVE EXPERIENCED in the intervening years between my birth and now is yet another sea change in basic American culture, especially since World War II. There was a lot of deprivation during the Great Depression and the Good War, this we know. People "tightened their belts." As a child, we had little, but what little we had was not wasted. We were connected to the earth, to the seasons, and to the night and day. We knew where our food came from and that it was important to walk in balance with nature, to give as much as we took, and to hold each other's hands as we journeyed along.

In the last 50 years or so we have lost our connection to the land. When we talk about a blackberry, we immediately think of a tech tool and not a sweet-tasting, dark-colored berry that helps sustain our very lives. We can actually live without the tech tools, believe me, but not without food that comes in the form of berries, fruits, and veggies. Everybody knows the Nike® swoosh symbol. How many people are left who can recognize the swooshing sound from the wings of a Sandhill crane flying overhead? When we lose our connection with what gives us life we can treat our earth as a product and not as a life-giving mother. Big difference, no?

How did we come to believe that happiness comes from buying more things? Who taught us that "shopping until we drop" is what life is all about? I see t-shirts now and then with the logo, "Born to Shop." Can we ever buy enough plastic things from China to fulfill what our hearts long for: rest, security, quiet times, peace,

No place to park your car, but this garage does have room for a few more things.

intimacy, sense of belonging, feeling connected, and love? Has our consumer society—driving the right car, drinking the right wine, wearing the latest fashion, living in a huge house—made us happy as promised? Can it be that if we have more material things to lose we feel more fear? Is it fear that keeps us in this consumer game? There are other ways to measure our own and our country's health and happiness than by how much we consume. Maybe we should ask how much we would be worth if we had no money.

I lived in South America for a time. People in Chile have a saying that I used to hear now and then: *Ustedes, Norte Americanos, saben como existir. Nosotros, Chilenos, sabemos como vivir.* "You who live in North America know how to exist. We Chileans, we know how to live!" Could be some truth in that statement.

The problem with owning things is that we have to care for them. We end up with the things owning us. First we have to work and earn money, or use one of our many credit cards, to buy them. We can, and many do, spend a lifetime cleaning, repairing, painting, and guarding our possessions while all the time buying more. I saw a store advertisement once: "We have more than 40,000 items to choose from. You can shop forever and never buy the same thing twice!" Whoopee! Let the fun begin! When will we ever have enough? Not only are people's houses full of, let's call it junk, but their garages are too. Who parks a car in their garage these days?

And what happens to all these treasures when we die? Our children don't want them. They already have their own piles at home. They take our stuff to a landfill, a thrift store, or stack it on the front lawn for a yard sale. If we could figure out a sharing system, not everyone in a city block would need their own lawn mower, boat, swimming pool, and a thousand other items that clog our lives, homes, garages, and storage units.

Speaking of storage places, recently three new large self-storage buildings sprouted in our coastal town. All three of these units are within eight blocks of our Walmart® super store. My feeling is that they were built close by so that shoppers could take their new purchases straight to a storage place without first passing them through their house. Sort of like a Monopoly® game.

It seems obvious that we might ask ourselves what it is that brings happiness into our lives. I leave you with a saying I heard years ago: "Every one of us wants to be happy. The price we have to pay for happiness is generosity." You can look at this as just a trite saying, or maybe it has a deeper meaning about how we should conduct our lives? I'll leave you to decide. 🦋

"No social system will bring us happiness, health, and prosperity unless it is inspired by something greater than materialism."

—Clement Attlee

CHAPTER TEN

The
Habitat House

IN THE MID-1990S, I recall listening to a radio program that was talking about a Children's Bill of Rights. Children from around the world had sent in letters offering suggestions for this program. One letter in particular grabbed my attention and remains vivid in my memory. A 14-year-old boy wrote, "Every child should have a blanket and a place to lie down and sleep!"

The last time I was in the Philippines was 1998. I read in their main newspaper, *The Manila Times,* that 25,000 abandoned children were living on the city streets, scrounging for food in landfills. I have walked these streets and the streets of other cities and seen groups of children huddled together, sleeping in doorways without a blanket in sight: throw-away children. A recent census in Los Angeles found more than 90,000 people living on the streets of that city.

Homeless children, living in shacks, look for food and saleable scraps of metal on a heap of garbage in Manila.

Many of these are parents with children, real children with their own hopes and dreams.

These are our children homeless on our streets. There are thousands of them. Strange world we live in, where dogs and cats often receive better treatment than our children. Welcome to America. Let's go shopping for pet food.

HABITAT FOR HUMANITY (HFH) is a nonprofit organization that works to care for others and provide sleeping places for both adults and children. They do their best, but they are losing ground. Many families, children and all, fall through the cracks in our system, as they say, where profit rules. The trouble with the profit system these days is that it seems to be profitable only for a few.

The need for decent, affordable housing in this country and throughout the world continues to increase. This is especially true as 83 million new people are added to this planet every year. Every one of these new human beings needs food, water, a blanket, and a place to sleep. Millions of families in our country spend way over one-third or even one-half of their income on housing alone. I know middle-class families with steady incomes who work and struggle, first to purchase a home and then to make their mortgage payments on time. In 2008, foreclosures in California alone peaked at 236,000. Money that used to go toward medical care, food, and a child's education is now spent so families can keep a roof over their heads.

Since coming to Oregon 15 years ago, we have built 20 Habitat houses here in our community. All across this country and in many other countries, people like you and me are working with our neighbors to build affordable housing with needy families. Habitat is not a give-away program; rather, it offers people a "hand up, not a hand out." So in addition to taking on an interest-free mortgage, the new homeowners have to put in 500 hours of "sweat equity," working with us volunteers to help build their home. Because we work mainly with volunteer labor from all walks of life—men, women, young and old, skilled and unskilled—we are able to build these houses for about $60,000, including land. This results in a mortgage that even low-income families can handle. (I know that land is more expensive in the cities, which will make mortgage payments higher.)

Many years ago I have to admit that I was not supportive of the seemingly endless calls for volunteers or for donations to different groups. Weekly, I would get letters asking for my help or money from organizations like the Disabled Veterans of America, Paralyzed Vets, Habitat for Humanity, the Cancer Society, the American Red Cross, and even our local schools—the list is long.

Then one day, to keep from falling into cynicism, I realized that volunteering and donating really weren't about helping others as much as a chance to help myself. We are a social people. We don't live in isolation from others. It is my experience that in reaching out to others we actually benefit who we really are.

And who are we really? What feeds our spirits and our hearts? What do I need to be whole? What gives meaning to our lives? Is it continued self-indulgence or sharing what we have with others? We all know that there is no guarantee we will be here tomorrow and that we can't take it with us when we go. Though I did see a cartoon recently showing a hearse being followed by a U-Haul truck. Good luck!

A HABITAT HOUSE, or any decent house, needs to be built so it doesn't leak either water or air. We take care to ensure that there are no holes under the siding that could let in moist air that can cause mold and rot, compromising both health and home and

Habitat houses are built by teachers, firemen, artists, bank tellers, mothers, cooks, and nurses. Men and women from all walks of life take time to help others.

increasing energy use. All walls are covered with 4×8 sheets of OSB and 30# felt paper before the siding is installed. Further care is taken to ensure that these new houses are not full of toxic fumes, which can come from paint, carpet, and a host of other common, seemingly innocuous materials. We work to make the home energy efficient, well ventilated, and comfortable; built from safe, health-preserving materials that require a minimum of upkeep and maintenance. We try to build from forest products and other materials that are renewable and sustainable so that we don't lay further waste to our homeland. Anyone building a decent, affordable house can do this. What it takes is a desire to learn, a willingness to be helpful, and the energy to make a difference. That is what we volunteers working with Habitat for Humanity try to do.

Besides helping others, many volunteers I have worked with have seen their experience as rewarding to themselves. I recall a young woman, a senior in high school, who arrived at our job site one summer with hammer in hand. She worked with us for several months, learning the basics of house building. For years now she has been a contractor in northern Oregon.

I have known many builders who look upon the local building department and their inspectors as the enemy. Habitat house builders, especially those without a lot of construction experience, can see them as a valuable resource. Many volunteer builders benefit from the knowledge these people have to help them build a safe, durable house that doesn't leak, isn't a fire hazard, and can stand up to daily use by an active family. If we go to our local building department with the right attitude, getting the needed permits to build should not be a major event. My mother long ago taught me that a good attitude would take me a long way no matter where I went or what I did. Arrogance and hostility seem to breed just that, arrogance and hostility.

Here on the coast we build Habitat houses on a stem-wall foundation rather than on a concrete slab. It's not a good idea to use a slab if you are building on an expansive soil like clay. Once the foundation is in place, we install treated posts to support the girders that hold the floor joists. This lumber is treated because of problems with termites and from mold and rot that can happen here in this wet, rainy climate. The new treated lumber seems to work well, but I'm not sure it's any safer than what we were using back in the 1950s. They ended the use of arsenic and increased the amount of copper. For years copper has been known as a carcinogen.

The old-growth forests are mainly gone. Now they harvest smaller, fast-growing plantation trees. These are cut up and glued together to form many products, like the 4×8 sheets of OSB. We use these sheets, replacing plywood, to cover the floors, roofs, and walls of our Habitat houses. Other manufactured products include joists that replace 2× dimension lumber, gluelams used as headers and beams, glued-together siding that replaces solid cedar siding, and even wall studs. The joists we use to form the house floor are manufactured; called Trus Joists®, they are glued together from laminated wood stock. Once the OSB sheets that form the floor are secured to these joists with a bead of adhesive and screwed in place, they should never squeak again (though I rather miss squeaky floors—they used to be a signal that your teenager was returning home late at night).

Working with volunteers offers a good chance for us to use salvaged and recycled materials. The main reason for this opportunity is, quite frankly, money. As volunteers, we are working off the time clock. Many salvaged products can be used in construction and should not be sent to a landfill. The problem is that these items usually take longer to install than a brand-new product. On one house we built, we milled salvaged cedar siding with a table-saw to create interior trim, casings, baseboards, and windowsills.

I recall doing an extensive home remodel for a family, where we put a second floor on their home. They were quite happy that they would get to use some old doors they had salvaged out of a hotel that was being torn down. They were nice doors, true, but it took three or four times as long to clean, repair, and install them. The family appreciated our efforts and could afford the extra money to pay for the additional labor.

> **"One of the joys of building a Habitat house is that you get to work with and know a new family."**

One of the joys of building a Habitat house is that you get to work with and know a new family. We build more than houses. We develop close friendships as we work side by side, taking breaks together, and sharing our stories. I will let the story of a young teenager, Ashley, tell you what I mean by this: "Contrary to what people may think, having a lot of brothers is not always fun. I know. I am the only girl in a family with six children. We used to live in a small house with two bedrooms. My parents and baby brother slept in one of the bedrooms. The other bedroom was for my four older brothers and me."

I remember Ashley when we were building her family's four-bedroom, 1,150-sq.-ft. house. Long before the house was ready for them to move in, she used to come and stand in the little room that was for her—her own bedroom—and just look around. She told me that with her own special room she would be able to invite her school friends over to visit. I heard later that after they moved in, she went from being a C student to an A student in her high school and was able to go on to college. All this because she had a place to study. That is what Habitat for Humanity is all about.

A big part of building an affordable house is to build small. Habitat houses are around 950 sq. ft. for a two-bedroom and 1,100 sq. ft. for a three-bedroom. Do we really need our bedroom to be the size of a discotheque? It is great to dance, but usually, though not always, we go to our bedroom to sleep for eight hours.

WALL FRAMING IS FUN for volunteers. They see immediate results from their work. People of all ages and abilities come to Habitat sites wanting to help. It is important that the site leaders be well organized so that when volunteers arrive everyone will have something to do. This is not always easy on a small house. Volunteers who arrive at a disorganized site are not liable to return. They come to help, give of themselves, and be productive, which makes everyone feel needed and happy.

The skill of cutting rafters and building a roof is rapidly being forgotten. Instead, we use roofs trusses on these small houses that form both the ceiling joists and the roof rafters. These trusses are assembled in a factory and delivered to the job site. As a carpenter, I have laid out and cut rafters for a huge number of houses, but factory-built trusses make sense. For one, they use less wood. Rafters spanning long distances often are cut from 2×8s or larger. Most all house roof trusses can be built from 2×4s. It takes much less skill for these trusses to be set in place and braced to make them structurally strong.

Unlike living in a small Habitat house, the trend in our country has been away from affordable housing. I have heard real estate agents and bank officials advise clients to build large because it will increase the resale value of their house. So we wind up building a house either to inflate our egos or to see if we can make a profit. We somehow got away from building what our family really needs. We might ask what owning and living in a huge house will do, not only to our earth, but also to us. Does a house with six bedrooms guarantee that we will have a close-knit family that loves one another?

Volunteers, including family members, are key to building affordable housing.

I was in a newly built house recently that had a huge "great room" with a high, vaulted ceiling that looked to be impossible to heat. These caverns used to be called living rooms. In my experience, living rooms were actually important in times past, when large families would gather together on a regular basis. Today, it seems to me, big rooms like this are used mainly to walk across to get to smaller spaces like the kitchen, a bedroom, or a bathroom. Most people seem to gather where actual living is taking place, like in the kitchen-dining area or in smaller rooms to relax and rest, watch TV, listen to music, text friends, or do homework. The Habitat houses we build have a kitchen-dining area that is open to a living room with a vaulted ceiling. This makes for adequate room when the family gathers to eat or talk about their day. Yes, some families still take time to do this.

Habitat houses that we built years ago were sheathed on the outside with lapped cedar siding, a traditional siding in the Northwest. After a time, I noticed that many of the boards covering the walls of these buildings were not lying flat. They were cupping and curling along their length. I realized that this siding was from second- or third-growth trees with large growth rings that left the siding unstable.

Manufactured fiber-cement siding has been around for a long time. It fell out of favor because it was rather brittle and hard to work with, and it was full of asbestos. These days, because high-quality wood siding is no longer available, fiber-cement siding is being used on all types of houses across our country. This time around it is free of asbestos.

Fiber-cement siding is not the perfect product. It takes a good amount of energy to produce it. Other than that, it seems to be pretty environmentally friendly. It is easy to install, termites won't eat it, it holds paint well, it is fire resistant, it won't decay, rust, mold, cup, or curl, it looks like wood lap siding, and it has a 50-year guarantee. What more can you ask for? All of this, but especially its durability, makes it an eco-friendly product. I

Using trusses to build roofs simplifies what used to be a more challenging job.

checked to make sure that the wood fiber used to make our siding came from a sustainable forest. I offer one caution. If you are cutting this material with a circular saw, the air will be filled with silica dust. It is not good for the lungs to breathe in ground-up sand. So wear a good mask, use a dust collector on your saw, or cut with shears that don't produce dust.

In the last 20 years or so, tool manufacturers have given us new tools for just about every construction task. There is an air-operated nail gun just for securing fiber-cement siding to a wall. We use a laser level to set our elevation grade when beginning a new Habitat house. Chop saws and sliding compound miter saws have many uses on a job site, from cutting rough 2× blocks to doing fine interior trim work.

The biggest change has been in cordless tools. Small batteries that hold a good charge are now available, so you no longer have to hook your tool to an electric power source and drag a cord around as you move from place to place. Battery-operated screwdrivers, for one, are seen on every job site. They have changed from being a novelty to being a real production tool.

PROVIDING A NEW FAMILY with four walls and a roof is just the first step in helping them get established. Many Habitat groups offer continuing education on how to be a homeowner. Remember that most of these families have always been renters, with little need to familiarize themselves with everything that goes on to keep a house in good repair or to know how a house works from top to bottom. So classes are offered on items like the actual care of the house: how to shut off electric power, water, and gas, change batteries in smoke detectors, drain sediment from the water heater, and check for excessive moisture in the attic, to name a few. They also teach how to use ecologically friendly products made from natural ingredients, how to conserve energy, and how to recycle. Good information needed by all of us in this world of diminishing resources.

In areas where the local city codes will allow it, as in our city, Habitat doesn't build a garage. They put it simply: "We build for people not cars." This, of course, reduces the total cost and makes the house mortgage lower. On the other hand, off-street parking is provided.

As we know, garages are mainly used to store stuff most of us really don't need. A Habitat home doesn't come with lots of storage other than closets. We trim the closets in our houses with more than just a shelf and pole to add some storage space. Hopefully, this minimal storage space is an encouragement for homeowners to do something with their lives other than shop.

Not every Habitat building is a success story. People in Habitat houses are like the rest of us in this society. Some have bigger problems than others. We had recently helped a family build their home and were building another in the same area. I walked across the backyard of the occupied house to get some nails from our tool shed parked nearby. Not long after that, a police officer pulled up at our job site and said that I had been turned in by the family and accused of trespassing. He gave me a lecture on violating other people's "sacred" property. Fellow volunteers were laughing,

One family at a time, Habitat for Humanity offers a hand up.

wondering if I would be led off in hand-
cuffs. Maybe I am the only volunteer in
the history of Habitat that helped build a
house for a family and then was accused
by them of being a trespasser. A year or so

"Garages are mainly used to store stuff most of us really don't need."

after that, this family had to be evicted because of repeated viola-
tions of neighborhood and city codes. I felt sad about that. I felt
especially sad because they had two young children who became
my friends during the building process.

But these happenings are the exception, not the rule. Most new
owners are happy and proud to have their own home. They had
been living in such hard financial straits that even to dream about
dreaming of being a homeowner wasn't possible. In the main,
people work hard to keep their homes and yards in good shape and
are assets to their communities.

WHEN WE MOVED INTO OUR PRESENT HOME,

the living room floor was covered with an ancient yellow 1950s shag
carpet. There were things growing in that carpet that even my
wife's dog didn't like. I don't care for carpet. Unless you pay the
price for a natural-fiber carpet, it usually is made with materials
that emit toxic fumes. I know of no way that you can ever totally
clean all that can live amongst the fibers—fleas, dirt, dust mites,
bacteria, and other allergens. Besides that, after some years of use,
a carpet usually needs to be replaced and the old one is sent off to
the local landfill. It is not what I would call a green product.

Speaking again of my wife's dog, I am not a big fan of in-house
animals. This is doubly true when people have carpets on which
animals sometimes have to "relieve" themselves. Growing up in a
ranch area, we always had lots of animals. They were kept around
for utilitarian reasons, not to be cuddled and treated better than

we often treat each other. Chickens laid eggs and supplied us with food; horses were for riding and pulling farm machinery; our dog, Gus, warned us if there was a rattlesnake in the area; and our old gray cat caught mice and rats. They did what they were supposed to do and all of them lived outside.

We no longer use carpet in the Habitat houses we build here on the coast. We use either prefinished solid wood or an engineered product called laminate flooring. Before I bought these products, I called the distributor and inquired how much formaldehyde had been used during the process of making them. Breathing formaldehyde fumes even on a short-term basis can cause dizziness, nausea, headaches, and problems with breathing. It took some time, but I finally found products that were somewhat environmentally safe. Making a home green can be a challenge. A few years ago California passed legislation limiting the amount of formaldehyde in building products, which should benefit all of us as industry conforms to these standards.

Laminate flooring is volunteer friendly, as no one needs a lot of skill to work with it. Usually no nails are required to install it, as one piece unites with a snap to the next. The joints between pieces are tight, which leaves little room for any dirt to enter. The surface is covered with a hard sealant, making it easy to clean and care for. Even the less-expensive grades seem to hold up well under heavy traffic.

AFFORDABLE HOUSING. Is that an oxymoron, a contradiction in terms these days? In 1970 in Los Angeles, when my children were little, we bought a small, three-unit, Spanish-style apartment for $25,000. At that time 11 percent of people's income went for housing. Even in the 1990s, I was able to buy a small, one-bedroom house here on the coast for $30,000. It needed about

$7,000 worth of repairs. Five years later I sold it for $59,000. Now, 8 years further on, it is on the market for $137,000. What is going on here? Is it greedy homeowners and realtors, free-wheeling bankers, and profit-seeking loan agents that keep home prices out of range for most of us? Even with the huge drop in home prices these last few years, I know few people who are actually able to afford them. Today even my own children can't afford to buy a house. Middle-class families have been priced out of the housing market even when both partners are working. Maybe we need to go back to the straw bale house and the Quonset hut.

Part of Habitat's commitment to decent housing is to finish the job with landscaping that doesn't need constant care. This means that the family, along with the volunteers, is given a chance to think beyond a traditional lawn. I have to admit that I just don't care for lawns. Partly this is because I grew up where the prairie was our lawn. Maintenance was the responsibility of cows, goats, and horses. A lawn, if it is to look "proper," often needs to be treated with chemical fertilizers and pesticides that can pollute our water systems and may even affect our children's health as they play on them. And besides that, you need to own, take care of, repair, and store a lawn mower. My feeling is that if we have a longing for green grass then we can visit a park, a golf course, or a cemetery. Our taxes support people who care for our parks; take your golf clubs with you and go for a nice walk; and the dead won't mind if you wander around overhead. Respectfully, of course.

When we moved into our Oregon home there was quite a bit of well-manicured lawn that went with it. Now there is a small lawn and a lot of garden space where we grow fresh, organic veggies for ourselves and our neighbors. No matter where we have lived, we always raise a garden full of good things to eat for our bodies and beautiful flowers to refresh our spirits. Many Habitat homeowners do the same. If we have to pay for water, we might as well get an edible return on our money. My mantra? Dig up your lawn. Plant a garden.

We try to make the Habitat yards attractive and welcoming. Sometimes we set things off by putting in a simple curved sidewalk. At other times we use attractive paving stones that allow rainwater to seep through rather than laying down impervious concrete. It makes sense to landscape with native plants. They flourish with little care, and like the ocotillo, can be quite beautiful. Here on the coast we have the native rhododendron plant that paints the entire town with beautiful flowers of various colors each spring. Better to use plants that have called the land around you home for centuries than to bring in exotic plants that demand lots of attention. Spaces between trees and shrubs can be filled with tree bark or different kinds of rock. Coastal people like to use pieces of driftwood, which wash up on our beaches, in their yards.

A yard can be made attractive without planting a water-guzzling lawn, and there's no need to buy a lawn mower either.

Also, we encourage new homeowners to create a special place in their yard where they can sit and read or just be quiet. One family placed a bench under a tree where they could

> **"I grew up where the prairie was our lawn. Maintenance was the responsibility of cows, goats, and horses."**

kick off their shoes, rest, and watch their children play. Sometimes even a few well-placed rocks can turn a common corner into an uplifting area.

Habitat homeowners are invariably in awe that they will have their own place. It is beyond their wildest dreams—and also means they won't have to move frequently. When anyone of us stays in a place for a time, even though it may only be a small piece of land, this place can become rich with meaning. There is a presence in such a place that transcends what was there before: a dead rock, a lifeless wooden tree, a senseless wind. When we pause, take time to listen to our hearts, resting for a few moments, we realize we are home. We can name this land and know an inner peace, if only for the moment. When separated from it for a time, we long to return. It's the place we call home.

We are human beings and we know that we deserve more than we can ever get at a big-box store, no matter if we go there with a super-size shopping cart. They just don't sell what we really need. Happiness can't be bought. It is, as they say, an "inside job."

There is a natural rhythm to all and we can enter that space, which is really not outside ourselves. It is important not to neglect our inner lives, to do what it takes to bring us closer to the deepest and best part of ourselves. We always hope that living in their own home built by us volunteers will help Habitat families find this space.

As theologian Howard Thurman put it, "Don't ask what the world needs. Ask what makes you come alive, and go do it. Because what the world needs is people who have come alive." 🌿

"If we will have the wisdom to survive,

To stand like slow-growing trees on a ruined place,

Renewing, enriching it,

If we will make our seasons welcome here,

Asking not too much of earth or heaven,

Then a long time after we are dead,

The lives our lives prepare will live here."

—Wendell Berry, "WORK SONG, PART 2, A VISION"

CHAPTER ELEVEN

Small Houses

ONE OF THE GREENEST THINGS we can do in the building industry, "asking not too much of earth or heaven," is to build small. I hold no moral high ground, but I have never lived in a house that was more than 1,200 sq. ft. I prefer living in a small home, especially one that I can afford. It would be hard for me to pay the property taxes on a huge house. Besides, small houses are easier to clean, need fewer repairs, and cost less to heat or cool. Overall, they have helped to make my life a little less complicated.

Years ago, I helped build three small houses up a canyon in the Santa Monica Mountains filled with huge oaks and sycamore trees. (I am especially fond of the sycamore tree, a California native that can reach a height of 100 ft. or more. The older trees have sprawling branches that follow the contour of the earth. Their thin bark peels off to leave the trunk and branches looking like an old carpenter who has been working out in the sun too long.) Each house was

650 sq. ft., with two bedrooms on the back side. The larger bedroom was about 10 ft. by 15 ft. and the smaller 10 ft. by 10 ft., with a common bath between. The front part—living, dining, and kitchen—took up the remaining space, 12 ft. by 30 ft. These cold measurements don't do justice to how warm the inside felt. The house was finished with two bay windows, deep window sills, wood floors, high ceilings, and wall niches to hold statues, clocks, or flower vases. The steep-pitched roof made room for a sleeping loft in the smaller bedroom. The front had clearstory windows that let in extra overhead light along with an inviting, Craftsman-style porch.

I drove up the canyon months later. The three houses, nestled between the trees, looked like they belonged there. Like a soddy, they appeared to grow out of the earth. Years later, I drove up the canyon again to show the small houses to a friend. I should have known better and rested with my memories. The houses were gone along with the mighty oaks and sycamores. In their place were huge mansions with fences, locked gates, and cameras keeping a watchful eye on me. Good idea!

I might as well finish the story. Still later on, the hot, dry Santa Ana winds that blow in from the desert every year pushed a fire into the dense canyon brush. More than 300 homes were burned to the ground. Guess what? Nothing is forever, not even diamonds. Maybe it is best to base our happiness on what lies in our hearts.

The material goods we gather together are so fragile. What often takes a huge amount of time and effort to acquire can be gone in a moment with an accident, a fire, an earthquake, a tsunami, a tornado, or a flood. I recall what happened to a classmate when we were in graduate school. Besides going to school, he was holding down two part-time jobs. He told me he wanted to buy a new red Camaro so he could "pick up chicks." One day he led me out to the college parking lot to show off his prize car. A week or so later he told me his sad story. He was driving down Hollywood Boulevard and stopped at a red light. The car behind him failed to stop and shortened his dream car by a foot or so. He sat in his totaled car, put his head on the wheel, and wept.

The message is out: Our earth is not appreciative of our life-styles. Like water, it doesn't need us. We need it. Water and the earth will do fine without us. As Joseph Wood Krutch has said, "Both the cockroach and the bird would get along very well without us, although the cockroach would miss us most."

Across our country and around the world, there is a movement among millions to live more sensibly, to slow down some, to try to be present, and to make life meaningful. Many people call this the "green movement," taking responsibility for our homeland. We are being asked if our lifestyle is sustainable. Are we using more of our limited resources than we are giving back? How do we want to spend our precious lives?

I read recently about a 10,000-sq.-ft. LEED-certified house, built in Aspen, Colorado, according to green standards (LEED stands for Leadership in Energy and Environmental Design). What sounds wrong about this? I have a contractor friend who built an even larger house for a couple in California. He told me the owners built it because they could. What can you say to that? Blessed are those who build small.

I have respect for the LEED group. Following their list is one way to measure the greenness or sustainability of a building. The problem is, I don't see this list filtering down to the mass of us Americans. For that to happen, we need a simplified approach to greenness that, even though it is not perfect, is easy to understand, doesn't produce a huge increase in the cost of construction, and makes sense. As a friend said, "Who can afford all the 'green bling' the LEED list says I need in order to have a certified green home?" Their long list is not a huge motivator for most of us.

WHEN OUR CHILDREN WERE SMALL, my wife Renee and I bought a small 1930s Spanish-style house with three units. Our studio unit was sited perfectly, by accident I am sure. Big windows allowed the winter sunlight to enter and heat our living space. Our actual floor space was less than 500 sq. ft., with beautiful cabinet work and a bathroom of soft, blue tiles that was a work of art. The one bedroom was made usable during the daytime by folding the Murphy bed up and out of the way in its closet-size room. (These space-saving beds have been around since 1916; check them out online.)

To add a little more space for our growing family, we went to work on the partially excavated space below. Back to the pick and shovel! Once the dirt was removed, we poured a concrete floor and built some retaining walls from concrete blocks. This allowed us space for two small bedrooms for our children, each with a sleeping loft and separated from a slightly larger bedroom by closets. The space was perfect for nighttime use, easy to heat in the winter, and cool in the summer. I cut in new windows for ventilation and an escape route in case of fire.

Access to the downstairs was made by cutting out the floor of the Murphy bedroom and building stairs with two three-step winders. In tight spaces you can decrease the amount of room you need for a stairway by making use of a winder. Winders change stair direction by 90 degrees and are sort of like a circular stairway.

Along with all that, I made another even smaller room downstairs in an unused space between the units for a playhouse. Our two children and their friends still have fond memories of playing

Older houses often had small spaces, like this unused tower, that were part of their design. We lived in the front Spanish-style, 500-sq.-ft. apartment, opened the tower room above, and excavated for three small bedrooms below.

in their hiding space. After all, does not every child, maybe every person, need a secret hiding place where they can just be?

We didn't stop there. We had access to another exciting room. The front apartment where we lived had a tower that had been constructed simply as part of the overall design. I cut a hole in the outside stucco with a carborundum blade to check if there was usable space inside. There was indeed, measuring about 9 ft. by 9 ft. What a find! I cut another hole, 2 ft. by 2 ft., in the dining room ceiling and built a ladder straight up for access. I had to put in new floor joists because the existing ones were not strong enough to support any added weight. I cut in small windows and then paneled the walls inside. From the window facing west we could see the ocean 15 miles away. With a carpeted floor and lots of pillows, this room became a joy to use, filled with lots of laughter and memories.

WOULDN'T IT BE HELPFUL for all of us to experience how other people live throughout our world? Maybe we should encourage our students, as part of their education, to live and work for at least 6 months in another country. As our world becomes more and more populated, and our earth comes under more and more pressures, can we continue to build and live the way we have been doing?

I once lived in a city to the south of Santiago, Chile, with around 10,000 other people in a poor suburb. My home was quite small, just like everyone else's. I had to walk four blocks to go to a public toilet and even farther to line up and wait to fill my water jugs at a spigot. All the months I lived there, I only saw two or three cars. People were kind to me, often sharing what little they had: an egg, some bread, and a smile.

Back in this country, I was following an armored car carrying someone else's money that had a sign on the back: "Protect What

Two small 45-sq.-ft. rooms in this old house, one on each side of the entry, provided ample space for children to study and listen to music.

You Value." Great idea. So what do we value? I have had the good fortune to spend time with people who were dying. I say good fortune, because they taught me a lot about living.

"I have had the good fortune to spend time with people who were dying. I say good fortune, because they taught me a lot about living."

Never have I heard a dying person say, "Oh, I wish I had spent more time at the office." Being busy and making money can be addictive. Often when we spend our entire life making money, that's what we end up with—money. What I heard from people who were soon to cross over was that if they had their lives to do over again, they would have spent more time with their families, dancing, helping other people, soaking in hot baths, and taking a nap now and then. Yes, naps are not just for us elders and little toddlers.

I suppose all of us have sad tales to tell. My first wife Renee died of cancer. I was single for a few years until I married Mila 29 years ago. We are a "blended" family, with five children between us. In the 1980s, we were living in a small, 950-sq.-ft., three-bedroom house with one bath. This was a bit tough with three teenagers waiting for the bathroom in the morning, but we survived with most of our sanity still intact.

To remodel would have been expensive. We also knew that our children would soon be moving on with their own lives. So rather than add on to our home, we decided to make use of some unused spaces. Across the front of the house was a porch where people long ago used to sit and tell their stories. We enclosed this porch to make two small rooms, each 5 ft. by 9 ft. (45 sq. ft.), one on either side of the entryway.

The construction part was pretty simple, done with materials salvaged from different job sites. I rabbeted some 4×4 fir posts to hold recycled, tinted glass above the porch railings, which let in lots of light. I framed in two walls at the entryway to close off the porch rooms. Entry to these rooms was made by removing two 3-ft.-wide windows in the house and making them into doorways.

In one room we put a table and chairs. This became a quiet room where reading and homework could be done. In the second room we laid down three layers of carpet remnants on the floor and added bunches of soft pillows. This was used as a place to listen to music, talk with friends, or even take a nap. To my amazement, these two little rooms became the most used rooms in the house. They were warm, bright, cozy, and inviting.

BUILDING GREEN is more than following a long laundry list. Besides deciding to build small and using local or recycled materials, we can pay much more attention to design. In fact, the key to building a small desirable house is design. I encourage you to look at the websites of two friends, Sarah Susanka (sarahsusanka.com) and Ross Chapin (rosschapin.com). They have dedicated themselves to designing small houses and cohesive communities for people rather than for maxed-out profit. There is a difference between a boxy house with a square front and one that reaches out and invites you in with open arms. We really can design homes that are wholesome places to live.

Beyond that, there are simple things we all can do to cut down on our footprint as we live on Mother Earth. Proper placement of a house on a lot can allow us to use heat-giving sunlight. Solar hot water heaters make further use of our sun. Trees can be planted to help cool a house. Large overhangs help shield a house from the summer sun and let in the low winter sun. Building materials come in 2-ft. increments, like 4×8 sheets of plywood. A house that is 36 ft. 9 in. long can cause increased waste. The plumbing for the kitchen, utility room, and bath can be kept close together, decreasing both time and materials needed for installation. Gray water can be diverted to flush toilets or for watering garden or lawn. Proper weatherstripping on doors and windows and lots of insulation add little to construction costs. Gravel or mulch that allows rainwater to seep into the ground can be used on pathways rather than impervious concrete. Skylights that you can open welcome natural light and allow hot air to escape. A whole-house fan in the ceiling can replace hot air with cool as the day winds down. Low-flow faucets and double-flush toilets cut down on water usage. Timers on lights, hot water heaters, and thermostats so that you can control inside temperature levels will lower energy costs. These are things we can all do.

Simplicity can also save lots of money for a homebuilder. The progression, at least here in the West, has been toward more complicated styles of construction. This has involved engineers to ensure that the house will stay in place when the "big one" hits. Today you can find about as much metal in the form of connectors, straps, hold downs, and braces in a house as wood. I sometimes wonder if all of this promotes safety or just fills the pockets of hardware makers. I have inspected many tract homes after a strong earthquake. Yes, they did "rock and roll," but I never saw one that collapsed. The newer houses built with lots of metal connectors seem too rigid to me. They often just split apart. Not being an engineer, all I can say is that simplicity has its value.

Besides our new porch rooms, we decided to convert part of our one-car garage into a bedroom, measuring 12 ft. by 13 ft. I framed a wall in the front section of the garage, leaving room for a small shop. In the back section, I added a sleeping loft by running a 4×12 beam from wall to wall and filling in behind with floor joists. This became the sleeping space for Eric, one of our children.

Actually, this construction strengthened the entire structure. I was able to take the sag out of the rafters in the gable roof, which were too small to carry the roof load. I cut in extra windows for ventilation, put in an entry door at the back, insulated the walls and ceiling, and covered them with drywall. Once the painting was finished, Eric had a "cool" bedroom all his own.

When I first started living in Spanish-speaking countries, friends would sometimes say that it would be a culture shock for me to be there. The culture shock I always experienced was when I came home, back to America. Yes, people in other countries were often quite poor in material goods. But all of that felt like home to me coming from the days of the Great Depression. Their houses were small, their food simple, and they often scrubbed clothes by hand, but they had community.

Every time I returned to this country, I was always taken aback by our waste and our haste. We throw enough food away on a daily basis to feed half of Mexico. Our houses are big enough to accommodate an extended family, not just a couple and their dog. I find that even something as simple as buying toothpaste is complicated when the store offers three dozen choices. On top of that, we often race around on our freeways and in our lives like the "end is near." That is culture shock for me.

ONCE THE CHILDREN HAD LEFT HOME, we sold our house and bought an old fixer-upper duplex not many blocks away. The owner, Alice, was a long-time friend and a committed shopper who wore a big, wide-brimmed hat and floral dresses. She had filled the living spaces of both units with items from endless shopping sprees. When I say that her two-story house was filled, I mean filled. For the last six years of her life she had to live and sleep on her front porch because there was no room in her house. Out on her overcrowded porch, she went to the bathroom in one-gallon plastic bottles that once held her drinking water. And yes, I have to say that about every two months or so I would pick the plastic bottles

This old house was condemned by the city and scheduled to be torn down.

up, put them in my pickup, and take them to a job site dumpster. Is this called being a devoted friend or a person having trouble with sanity?

The roof leaked badly, so water destroyed everything inside the house, including huge stacks of the *Los Angeles Times,* piles of clothes in her wardrobes, the grand piano, oak flooring, beds—all expensive, all rotted. I was reminded of a saying: "When you find yourself in a hole, stop digging." She kept right on digging; right on shopping.

The city had condemned the house to be torn down, but I got them to grant me a remodeling permit. This seemed to be a green thing to do—restore an old building. Just think of the energy needed to build it in the first place. There would have been much more energy used to tear down the building and start over than to restore it. To begin, we hauled eleven large commercial containers of her accumulated belongings to the landfill.

"Shopping is here to stay. What needs to be looked at is what and why we buy."

There are many more stories to tell around her and her life spent in shopping malls. Once when she was living on her porch, someone broke into the downstairs apartment and stole some items. She asked me to go with her to see what was lost. I opened the door and we crawled on our hands and knees over piles of stuff that were at least 4 ft. deep. She went to the bedroom, opened a dresser door, pulled a gold watch with a diamond-studded band out from a stocking and said: "At least they didn't steal this." She put the watch back in the sock, wrapped it, and tossed it back in the drawer. As we were crawling out to leave, she mentioned that someone had stolen a painting of lilacs from a wall. She swore a bit, "Those bastards," and then said, "Oh, they can't be all bad. At least they love lilacs!"

Shopping is here to stay. What needs to be looked at is what and why we buy. We can begin to ask informed questions about where a product was made and by whom. Was it made by underpaid or child laborers working in squalid conditions? Will what we buy outlast the one-year warranty? Can it be repaired or just thrown away? Is what we are buying causing harm to Mother Earth? Do we really need this product? I once attended a wedding party for friends who received, among other gifts, 18 kitchen appliances. They returned all but 3 to where they were purchased.

THE ONE-CAR GARAGE alongside the battered house we were remodeling was also rotting and falling down. Alice had stored her mountain of wedding gifts from 1945 inside, closed the door, and never opened it again. I knew this woman well and loved her. She was just a little more eccentric than most of us. Just a little. We tore down the old garage and salvaged what we could.

With the foundation gone, I excavated and built a small room under the garage. The joists became the deck of this garage and the ceiling of my writing room.

This building was on the side of a hill, so I got a permit to build a room underneath. We excavated and built block walls as a foundation for the garage. This room, 8 ft. 6 in. wide and 14 ft. long, was a perfect writing place for me. It was quiet and protected like a dugout, with two sides backed up to dirt and the other two sides shaded from the summer sun by a big pecan tree. I put in two corner windows where I sat to write.

Right outside my door, I would sometimes sit and relax with my wildflowers and plants and listen to the mourning doves and mockingbirds. They started singing before daybreak. The mourning dove has a mournful coo that mimics the cry of the wind. The mockingbird sings like there are 20 different birds around. They want you to know: "Wake up time! I'm here. I sing. Get used to it!" I wrote my first book there in 1989. I still miss that little place. It's part of me.

Building green means we need to take into consideration the impact our home will have on our health—physically, mentally, and spiritually. A well-designed house can nurture and heal us. Small doesn't have to mean cramped, uncomfortable, or ugly; we can design our living spaces to be uplifting.

The urban sprawl that we have known up until now has been extremely profitable to a few, but maddening for many of us. It is no longer sustainable to build a single-family dwelling on a large plot of land. Having to travel long distances to work via an oft-clogged freeway, one person per car, can take hours out of our day and affect our mental well-being, adding more anxiety to our already stressed-out lives. Road rage becomes understandable in such situations. How can it make sense that we have to drive several miles just to buy a loaf of bread at an ugly strip mall that should never have been built in the first place? Neither the gasoline-driven automobile nor strip malls are sustainable in the long run.

Whenever I became weary writing, I could refresh myself by sitting amongst the flowers right outside my writing room door.

We all know that we can do better than this. We can order our lives in a way that is kind both to our earth and to ourselves.

> "How can it make sense that we have to drive several miles just to buy a loaf of bread at an ugly strip mall that should never have been built in the first place?"

The most sustainable type of transportation is not to drive anywhere at all. We should be able to live in communities where we can walk or bike to most of what we need: jobs, food, theaters, parks, recreation, churches, libraries, the houses of friends, and so on.

I have trust in ourselves that we do have the knowledge and ingenuity to build living places that are beautiful and fun to live in. I know we can do it, because I have seen it done here and in other countries. Whole cities and even nations have plans to get off fossil fuels and build millions of houses that consume zero energy for communities of people that are moving in the direction of self-sustainability. The task is huge, but we Americans have faced huge tasks before. We need to educate ourselves about where we have been, what we have done wrong, and what a sustainable world will look like. If need be, we can forgive ourselves for our mistakes, roll up our sleeves, and do what we know we can do. It will mean re-ordering our priorities to keep our children, our descendants, and our fragile world going on for a long, long time. Is this not a patriotic thing to do?

WHAT I MISSED MOST when we moved to coastal Oregon from California 15 years ago was our clothesline. (It is probably not news to you that the Northwest is wet and rainy.) Maybe it comes from my childhood. I love to hang newly washed clothes on the line. It gives me time to listen to the bird sounds, think, and just be. The added benefit is that when I bring them back into the house I get to breathe in the soft, warm smell of sun-dried clothes.

Another small space (10 ft. by 10 ft.) that served as an extra bedroom when children visited. I wrote my second book in this room.

This coastal area was dominated for years by big timber mills and by commercial fishermen. Coos Bay is a deep-water port and was at one time the largest lumber-shipping center in the world. It also had hundreds of fishing boats. The endless stands of big timber have been gone since about 1980, and the massive salmon runs—so huge that you could hardly see the water in the mile-wide bay—started disappearing a few years later. The area around has become mainly a retirement community, as workers had to leave looking for jobs. Recessionary times are not new to these coastal residents.

We moved to this area because it has great beauty, to be near a brother, a sister, and a daughter, and because housing was inexpensive. As I mentioned before, we bought a small, one-bedroom house for $30,000. What our little house lacked, and what I needed, was a room in which I could write another book.

"I think that most of what has been done to our world, our earth, has been done out of ignorance and not ill will."

The city code here allows you to build a room, 10 ft. by 10 ft. (100 sq. ft.), without getting a permit. That sounded good to me. In the backyard near my garden, we poured footings for piers and set the floor joists on them rather than on a full foundation. The rest was rather simple: framed walls, truss roof, shingles, a door, two windows in my writing corner, siding, and a coat of paint. Once the inside was finished, I set up a plywood desk, fired up my computer, and started writing my second book in a small, quiet, peaceful place. We built a walkway between the house and the room. It also doubled as a sleeping room when children came to visit.

It was in my writing room that I became aware of a new smell. I am an early riser and like to write in those morning hours when all is quiet, the sky often lit by the glow of the moon. The smell I caught drifted in though an open window carried by the morning breeze. I know that night-blooming jasmine grows in many places in our country. Maybe I just never slowed down long enough to let it embrace me. I apologize to this plant for that; it must have asked me to wake up many times before. Up close, I find the smell coming directly from the tube-like flowers is almost overpowering and not all that appealing. But getting a whiff blown in from a distance "knocked my socks off." Nature offers constant surprises if we keep our eyes, ears, and nose open to what she has to offer.

I think that most of what has been done to our world, our earth, has been done out of ignorance and not ill will. Sometimes we have to learn the hard way that what we have been doing serves neither our planet nor ourselves. Do we really want to live in an economy that survives only if we continue to buy more stuff? When we hear that "consumer confidence" is down, that we are not doing our duty and buying more things, that the stock market has fallen several hundred points, how do we feel? Are we being patriotic Americans?

I have had to learn the hard way many times in my life. I recall that when I was an invincible 14-year-old I felt I could do anything without serious consequences. What a glorious age! I was out riding my battered old bicycle doing what boys do—taking exciting chances. Coming down a hill like a bat out of hell, I had no doubt that I could jump and clear a ditch at the bottom. Wrong! I wound up with my bike in a crumpled heap on the far side and me with a broken right leg. I spent weeks in a cast and then graduated to crutches. That's what we call learning the hard way, no?

We have long been taught to think that our supply of fossil fuel is endless, that everyone should have an automobile and be able to drive forever if that is what they choose to do. Individual freedoms encourage us to do whatever we want, often without thought of the consequences for our neighbors or the world community. This is my right so get out of my way! Do we always have to learn the hard way? For example, our mass transit systems have, for the most part, been gutted. As a result, the air in our cities is filled with the toxic fumes of millions of automobiles, leaving us with many cases of respiratory problems, especially among

Learning the consequences of my actions— and that I am not invincible.

our beautiful children and our old folk. The cost of building roads, bridges, and highway infrastructure is no longer sustainable. Every year in our country there are millions of auto accidents causing hundreds of thousands of injuries along with more than 35,000 deaths of our fellow citizens. What's wrong with this picture? It is almost safer to catch cancer than to go out for a drive.

We have been living in our present home for 12 years. Once again, it is small, with two bedrooms, a 950-sq.-ft. house built in the 1950s that is more than adequate for the two of us. Actually it is a special place, easy to care for, and fairly energy efficient, especially after I replaced the single-pane windows and insulated underneath the floor and in the ceiling. It has good windows to the east and south. The view up the Coos River and on to the low-lying hills of the coastal range miles away is outstanding. We can sit in our living room and watch the sun rise and name the birds at our feeders: the nervous pine siskin, American goldfinch, chickadee, purple finch, chatty junco, Stellar jay, Townsend warbler, white- and golden-crowned sparrow, streamlined oriole, and many others that fill our morning air with music.

When we moved in we inherited a rickety, battered, part-wood, part-concrete deck on one side. The flashing was rotted, allowing water to leak into the downstairs bedroom. I removed and salvaged the wood part of the deck. Breaking up the concrete section into sizeable blocks was real work. I thought maybe an acquaintance could use the blocks to build a retaining wall for a garden spot at his place. When I inquired about this he said no, he didn't need them but he knew someone who could use them to fill in a wetland on his land. What do you say in a case like that? Fill in a wetland! Have we not learned the vital importance of wetlands in our lives? Is it in our genes that we always have to learn the hard way?

We live on a slight hillside. Once the deck was removed, I noticed that there was considerable space below that was filled with junk left by the previous owner. What I saw was the possibility of building a couple of small, quiet rooms there to make use of this unused space. It seemed to be better to have rooms rather than a place to store junk.

ONE OF THE JOYS OF BEING A CARPENTER is that I get to work with my hands and be creative. I have been building all my life. I don't care to build huge, custom homes, but I do enjoy building warm places, especially when I can use salvaged and recycled materials. I find it a joy to be able to create something usable while making an ugly space beautiful.

So I built two small rooms below the deck with this in mind. One is 7 ft. by 8 ft. that we use as a place to stretch out and as an extra bedroom when children come to visit. The other is 8 ft. by 9 ft. that I call a quiet, sacred room. The back wall for these rooms is the existing building. The front and side walls I framed with salvaged deck lumber. The roof-ceiling below the deck has a low pitch so rain water will run off. I had to buy the exterior siding to make it look like the rest of the house. I used some stained-glass windows that my wife bought at a yard sale to give the interior a special feel.

Inside the quiet room I built a bookshelf and a place to sit and read. The walls and ceiling are finished with local western red cedar from a contractor who had it left over on a big custom house he built. On the laminate wood floor is a wool rug given to me by a woman I helped. She had no money for the job I did for her, so she insisted that I take the rug. This, along with some cushions to sit on, gives the entire place a feeling of elegance fit for an old carpenter like me.

Two small, beautiful rooms snuggle into an unused space below our deck.

I use a cushion to sit on and do nothing, meditating quietly, paying attention to my breath, allowing the mind to be calm and present. One of the requirements on a construction site is that we be present. By this I mean more than being physically there. When we are working with equipment like power saws, routers, nailers, and forklifts we need to be mentally present all day long. The more we can be present, the safer the job will be for ourselves and fellow workers. I can say with assurance that every time I have been hurt at work it was because my mind was elsewhere.

I once worked with a framing partner, Paul, in the 1950s. Our job was to cut rafters and build roofs. Until about 10 in the morning when he finally woke up, he was dangerous to be around—"unsafe at any speed." He was not what you would call mentally present. I used to swing a long 2×4 around early on in the day and try to whack him in the shins to wake him up. It was a case of either him or me. Twice he dropped a rafter on my foot and broke a couple of my toes. Finally, one morning it happened. We were sheathing a roof and he, with his mind elsewhere, cut a huge gash in his forearm with a circular saw. This time it was him not me. The muscle was gaping open, spurting blood. I ripped a piece of cloth from my shirt, put a tourniquet on his arm, got him down from the roof, and drove him to an ER. That was the last time I saw Paul. I heard later that he joined the Fire Department. I wished them well.

Long ago the poet Rumi said, "Don't go back to sleep." Sitting in quiet meditation, doing nothing more than watching our breath, is a way to calm our rattle-on minds and help us to be awake in the present. Usually we are living in the past or thinking about what will happen tomorrow. We miss the only time we have—right now, this moment. We can train our bodies to be athletic. Well, we can also train our minds to be here, right here, present with family, bird sounds, with my wife's dog who tolerates me at best, and yes, even the wind.

The wind for a long time was my sworn enemy, pushing me this way and that, chilling me deep inside. It was in quietness one day that I realized that the wind is actually my sister. Sisters, especially the older ones, are here to give us a shove in the right direction at times. Knowing that they will always love us, I gave up. I just let go and surrendered. From then on it has been a free ride and what a ride it's been! In the words of Toni Morrison, "If you surrender to the wind, you can ride it."

I love to work, but I don't think any of us like working at a mindless job. We often do it because we need the money, but we don't like it. The self-gratitude we get from doing a well-done job that we like is real. This is especially true if we can dedicate ourselves to learning and practicing one of the fundamental arts of our lives: farming, teaching, cooking, nursing, parenting, lovemaking, carpentry, painting, and craftwork of all sorts. Working within one of these caring professions offers us a chance to experience a fulfillment that won't come with filling another shopping cart with plastic junk or pushing one more piece of paper in the office of a huge corporation.

In 1969 when our firstborn, Eric, was a baby, my wife and I spent some time living in a small town in Mexico. We had little money, but we lived simply. It gave us time to figure out what it meant to be parents and to just be with our new creation.

When we returned to our country it was still safe to hitchhike. We were picked up outside of El Paso, Texas, by a soap salesman working for Proctor and Gamble. During our ride to Albuquerque, he told us that his wife and he always wanted to travel, go camping, and have fun. He said that all they ever seemed to do was work and buy more things. He mentioned that two years ago they had bought a full set of camping equipment, set it up in their backyard, slept in it one night, and never used it again.

When he dropped us off he went to the trunk of his car and gave us a sack full of soap samples along with $20. He told us that it made him feel good to help us. Being with us for several hours in a closed car also probably convinced him that we all needed some of his soap. We thanked him, wished him well, gave him a hug, and stuck our thumbs in the air looking for a ride on to Denver. 🌿

I want to know

if you can be with joy

mine or your own

if you can dance with wildness

and let the ecstasy fill you

to the tips of your fingers and toes

without cautioning us

to be careful

to be realistic

to remember the limitations

of being human.

—Oriah Mountain Dreamer, "THE INVITATION"

CHAPTER TWELVE

The Greenhouse

LONG BEFORE WE WERE TALKING about green houses, we were making use of solar power to warm up our greenhouses. My father built a small cold frame on the south side of our house so my mother could get her seeds started early. The growing season in western Nebraska, before global warming, was 3½ months at best. I have often wondered where we would be today in energy use if we had incorporated solar power into our home construction way back in 1931. The basic technology was available, no? I recall, as a chilled child, sitting in a chair soaking up the sun's warmth and reading a book. This was better than standing in front of an old cast-iron kitchen stove. Maybe using the sun's endless, free power

> **"I have been a gardener all my life. I learned how to care for the soil and raise good veggies from my mother in the 1930s."**

didn't appeal to the equally powerful oil companies who wanted to sell us their petroleum products.

I have been a gardener all my life. I learned how to care for the soil and raise good veggies from my mother in the 1930s. Gardening there in those cold, dry times was a challenge compared to planting in southern California. There is some truth to the saying that all you have to do in that climate is to throw seeds at the ground, add some water, and let the warm sun do the rest.

Gardening on the Oregon coast presents a different kind of challenge. We do have a long growing season. Our winters seldom get below 40°F, so vegetables like kale, parsley, leeks, garlic, shallots, and chard can produce through March, when they finally go to seed. The problem is that our earth doesn't warm up enough to germinate seeds in March. Summer temperatures are never hot, seldom reaching 80°F. This is not the kind of weather you need to grow Nebraska corn, or juicy watermelons for that matter. Having a greenhouse meant that a ready-to-plant gardener could get with it long before the earth warmed up.

Thankfully, our property is small and easy to care for. I have other things to do than cutting and caring for a big lawn and a monster house. The same question arises: What is this short life all about? My Native American friends sum it up in one sentence: "Life is about walking in balance with all your relations." To walk in balance means that in whatever we do, we never take more than we give. Things get out of balance when we get greedy. Greed causes harm to all our relations.

I recall a 99-family-unit structure we framed for a developer in the West Valley with 3 or 4 bedrooms in each apartment. He advertised the finished product, saying that it had a playground for children. Upward of 300 children moved in, only to find a playground about the size of my living room with no swings, no jungle gyms, and not even any trees to shade them from the hot summer sun.

> "Things get out of balance when we get greedy. Greed causes harm to all our relations."

When we see our world as a lifeless object, we can mistreat it. Once I was at a Halloween festival with my family in a beautiful wooded area. We were parked behind a car with a familiar bumper sticker: "America, love it or leave it." The owner was in his car, opened the door, and dumped out a big tray of cigarette butts on the ground along with a few beer cans. Walk the talk, please. Saying "all my relations" means just that. Everything is alive, has energy flowing through it, just like us. This means we need to be mindfully aware that we are here in relationship to all and dependent on all for our very existence.

I have sat many times in a native sweat lodge. When the red-hot rocks are brought in the leader will often say, "Welcome grandfather. These are our oldest relatives. Listen to what they have to say. Learn from them." It goes without saying that our industrial, materialistic world does not promote this type of thinking.

This might be a good time to ask the biblical question, "For what shall it profit a man, if he shall gain the whole world, and lose his own soul?" It does seem legitimate to ask: What gives meaning to our lives really? What do we do that is fulfilling in our lives? In my wanderings, I find lots of confusion among people, dissatisfaction, depression, anxiety, and sadness. Well, planting and raising a garden, no matter how small, may not be a total solution to how we feel, but it does help. I can still see the wonder and awe in children's eyes when they see a seed they have planted peek up through the ground. I have spent time in areas of great material poverty and yet seen joy as people tended their small garden or watered a potted plant on a windowsill.

One of the reasons I garden is that I love fresh veggies and don't care to go to a supermarket. Those places are so huge that I fear getting lost inside and not being able to find my way out. Maybe I need to go there with a GPS. Heading down some of the aisles, I feel like I need a respirator to keep my lungs safe from breathing in toxic fumes. I didn't grow up with processed food, soft drinks, and sugary breakfast cereals. What I need to buy for myself could be shelved in a room about the size of our small local health-food store: vegetables, fruits, soap, nuts, whole-grain cereals, good bread, eggs from chickens that have actually seen the light of day, and yes, toilet paper. In the big markets I find row after row of items I just don't need. A Google search says that the number of different items in a mega-store can be well over 50,000! Is that true? If it is, that puts the stretch to my imagination. Does anyone else find this strange? I sit here searching for words to try and make sense of it all.

WHEN I WAS IN CALIFORNIA, I once lived in a house that was built in an old, seldom-seen style. It was a house built without wall studs, what some people call box framing. This is the way I built my little greenhouse tucked away on a back corner in full view of the morning sun.

When we moved into our present home, I knew there was a garden plot in the back. I asked the former owner, himself a gardener, how his growing experience had been. He advised me to use a good amount of chemical fertilizer if I wanted anything to grow. He also told me what pesticides to use to control the bugs and slugs that were eating his produce.

I realized I was in trouble when I turned over the first shovel of dirt in his garden space. The earth was dead! It had no earthworms. The first year the vegetables I produced were stunted. I

A compost pile can turn leaves, grass, and kitchen waste into valuable, nitrogen-rich fertilizer for your garden.

am used to a garden that is populated with birds, butterflies, bees, worms, caterpillars, garter snakes, and even slugs. Nothing was moving. It took me several years of composting and loving care to bring the soil back to life. I now have a compost pile in the back that eats up leaves, grass, garden scraps, and other organic matter and turns it into nitrogen-rich soil. My garden is smiling and the worms and butterflies have returned. Is there anything more delightful than having a beautiful butterfly around to brighten one's day? Granddaughter Julia, age 12, helps me take care of my garden. That girl can fly just like a butterfly!

To make room for the greenhouse, I had to clear out a section of laurel hedge that had been planted years ago. In California, I used to plant dozens of trees to keep our house cool and protected from the hot sun. Here on the coast we do just the opposite, praying for more sunlight.

My first step was to build a 6-ft. by 8-ft. floor. This floor, built close to the ground, was made from treated wood to preserve it from rot. Using untreated wood in this wet, high-humidity area is a recipe for disaster. It takes a few years, but eventually termites, bugs, and rot will weaken and destroy any untreated wood that is close to the earth.

One side of this platform rests on a concrete wall that marks the location of our property line. I poured two footings, 16 in. by 16 in., to hold concrete piers that support the other side. With the span only 6 ft., I was able to use 2×4 floor joists. I sheathed this struc-

Here are a few seedlings that are quite happy in their warm space.

ture with ½-in. treated plywood. Although 48 sq. ft. may not sound like much, I can start hundreds of little plants in this space and still have room for garden supplies.

Not far from where we live is a manufacturing plant that makes sheets of plywood. At one time this factory used wood from our long-gone, old-growth trees. Nowadays, the skins (thin sheets) peeled from trees that make up the layers of plywood are shipped in from other countries. This is the end of the road for some of the world's life-giving rainforests. The skins arrive loaded on pallets that are 4 ft. wide and 8 ft. long. The pallets are made mostly from mahogany boards. That's right, mahogany boards, enough to make a woodworker's mouth water. I bought 10 pallets for $2 each and dismantled them. All of the boards were a full 1 in. thick, up to 20 in. wide, and knot free! The 3-in. by 4-in. stringers under the boards were from other species of hardwood trees. Some of these I recognized as rosewood, which I made into jewelry boxes for gifts. Am I missing something? Should I find it hard to believe that such precious wood is being used for pallets?

I have read about the forests of the Amazon and other areas and how they are being clear cut. What can I say? It seems arrogant to me that we can think it is OK to cut down these huge forests, our relatives, and that life will go on as always. These forests are home to thousands of plants, animals, and even native people that will be lost forever. What can I do?

I have mentioned that we came from the earth, our Mother, and yet we behave like conquerors from another planet. We are here only because of our connection with plants, insects, bacteria, minerals, liquids, and sunlight. And still, we often work hard to destroy our world, devouring all in sight and leaving behind sewage, empty beer cans, garbage dumps, smog, and polluted water. For the life of me, I don't get it. My mother always told me not to make a mess of things for others to clean up.

My next task was to set up my tablesaw and rip the stack of mahogany boards down to 6-in. widths for the siding boards. I also ripped ½-in. by 2-in.-wide strips to use as battens to cover the vertical joints between the boards. Once I had all the wood well bathed in linseed oil, I was ready to build the greenhouse.

FARMER'S MARKETS ARE NOTHING NEW. I have seen them both here in our country as a child and all over other countries as a traveler. After the Good War, farmer's markets, along with the small farmer, basically went the way of the 5 bil-

Like two peas in a pod. Granddaughter Julia and I ready to sell veggies at our local farmer's market.

Single-wall construction starts by screwing boards to the outside of the floor frame.

lion passenger pigeons, at one time probably the most numerous birds in the world. It is not easy in this country to make a living as a small-time farmer. My own father tried it and lost out to dry weather, bank loans, and the rise of huge industrialized growers. Relics of local farm markets were seen as people sold their produce in roadside stands.

So it has come as a great joy to see farmer's markets sprouting up like carrots all over our country. Small farmers, bypassing the middleman, can charge a fair price for their produce. Those of us who buy at our local markets feel as if we are at least getting super-fresh food grown nearby and not flown in from Chile or even China. Markets are also a social event and not just a shopping job we have to do. Watch how customers interact with the farmers and with each other. By contrast, we go to a supermarket to get in and get out and not to stand around and chat.

The next step in my greenhouse building job was to cut to length the 6-in. boards to build the side walls. I cut them at 82 in. long. Here is where this old style of building eliminates the use of wall studs. I screwed the boards flat against the outside of the wood floor, using galvanized screws that resist rusting and making sure the boards were plumb, straight up and down. Builders are using more and more screws these days along with battery-operated screw guns. Nails on a job like this won't, in the long run, have the holding power of a screw.

For the top plates, I used two 10-ft. 4×4s, letting them cantilever 2 ft. out over the door on one end to form a little porch. For the ridge, I used a 4×6 that also cantilevered out 2 ft. I put a 14-degree rip on the top edge of these beams to fit the 3-in-12 slope of the roof. Midway up on the wall boards, I screwed them to a flat 1×3 board to stabilize the wall and to act as a sill for the windows. Then it was just a matter of filling in the end spaces and under the windows with more 6-in.-wide boards.

One thing that has thankfully happened in our country is that there is now more salvaging and recycling of construction materials. In Los Angeles, I often saw beautiful old houses destroyed in a day by a bulldozer. Hand-made doors, curved stairs with irreplaceable railings, invaluable stained-glass windows, hand-crafted cabinetry, old-growth studs and joists were all treated like garbage, broken up, loaded into a dump truck, and hauled to a landfill. The reason given for not salvaging these items was that labor costs were too high. With the lot cleared, a Craftsman house could be replaced with a multi-unit, square-box apartment. "Money talks and BS walks," as the saying goes! I'm sorry, but thinking about it makes me sad. What do we value?

Our local community garden offers 60 separate plots to people who live in places where there is no place to plant.

I bought two single-glazed windows for $5 each at our local Habitat Re-store. These windows in their aluminum frames are easy to install. I set them on the sill and screwed them in place through a flange that goes all around the window. People in our area know that when they remodel or have construction items left over they can bring them to the Re-store and they will be used once again by people like me. I know a person who made a complete greenhouse by using nothing other than sliding glass doors that he bought at the Re-store.

Not only do people recycle more, but more people are planting their own backyard gardens or getting their hands into a plot of earth at a community garden. Some of us even get the chance to sell veggie items at our local farmer's market. My wife and I work for a farmer during the summer months. He lives in central Oregon in the valley east of the coastal range. I help him set up four canopies and many tables at 5:00 a.m. and take them down after 3:00 p.m. He brings in seasonal fruit and nuts: strawberries, peaches, nectarines, figs, plums, apricots, cherries, and blueberries, along with filberts, almonds, and walnuts.

I don't have a huge garden, but it produces more than the two of us can eat. Three years ago, we asked the farmer we work for if we could have a small spot on one of his tables among the fruit to sell our veggies. The first year, we sold $96 worth of fresh, organic, good-tasting carrots, onions, kale, spinach, chard, herbs, squash, cucumbers, and lettuce. The second year we sold $176 worth. This year, with the help of our greenhouse, we were up to $580. Not a fortune, but it does show how much you can grow from even a rather small, well-tended garden plot. It was lots of fun and shoppers had fresh, healthy food for their table. And for us, we received more than enough money to buy next year's seeds for the coming planting season.

It's no fun to be poor and hungry. Hardscrabble lives often mean that joy is hidden beneath fear of how we will care for our family, what will we do if we get sick, where our next meal will come from, and whether we will have a place to sleep this coming night. Fears of this sort are likely to become more common as the world's population continues

Plexiglas makes a good roof covering and lets in lots of sunlight.

to grow exponentially: 1950—2.5 billion; 2010—6.8 billion; 2050—9.3 billion? How will we be able to feed all of us in this climate-changing world? Will what is needed to live a productive, joyful,

fun-filled life forever be out of reach for the masses? And even if we have money, it is fair to ask: Will there always be food available for us to buy?

For the greenhouse roof, I bought two sheets of recycled Plexiglas®, $1/2$ in. thick by 4 ft. wide and 8 ft. long, for $10 each. I drilled a few holes in these sheets and screwed them to the ridge and to the 4×4 at the wall line. The Plexiglas worked perfectly for the roof, allowing good sunlight in to warm the room and help seedlings grow. The roof is 10 ft. long. I sheathed the last 2 ft. and sealed it off with dark shingles. The shingles absorb the heat from the sunlight, adding a bit more heat to this structure. To make the ridge cap watertight, I found a piece of 10-in.-wide aluminum siding, which I bent to the slope of the roof and sealed in place with caulking.

To cover the space between the vertical siding boards, I used the narrow batten strips. I screwed one of these strips over every joint and around the windows as trim to hide the aluminum flange. I made the door for the greenhouse out of the same 1-in. stock as the walls. The vertical boards are held together by horizontal and diagonal boards on the inside. I hung the door with a couple of metal strap hinges painted black to set them off; the door handle is made from a piece of driftwood I picked up on the beach. I fabricated a sliding door closure from the pallet wood. On the inside I built a potting table and storage shelf under one window, and some shelves at one end to store garden tools, pots, compost, and planting materials. The entire building, not counting my time, cost $86.

A different type of prehung door, made from the same
material as the greenhouse and hung in place with a
couple of strap hinges.

A couple of years ago, I decided to make our greenhouse look
like the rest of the house. First, I removed the battens. (Many of
these are now used as gardens stakes.) I bought seven 4×8 sheets
of grooved plywood that cost me a little less than $250, about
three times the cost of the original material. The Re-store supplied me with partial cans of paint to prime the back side and seal
it from excess moisture. I painted the front side the same color as
the house, cut the sheets to size, and screwed them to the vertical boards. I used some of the battens as trim at the corners and

around the windows. I admit to loving my little greenhouse nestled away in the corner. It means that my veggies have a warm home for an early start on the growing season.

WITH THE SCRAPWOOD LEFT OVER, I made a
classy, steep-pitched-roof doghouse for my wife's dog, Drala, a long-haired Dachshund rescued nine years ago. I actually like this dog and treat it kindly, but it is her dog, not mine. He has visible scars on his body from mistreatment. I suspect this was done by a man, because he barely tolerates me, barking whenever I come in the door. My only hope for peace and quiet is that I will outlive him. I am afraid to ask my wife to make a choice between the dog and me.

Are there other ways to live and be that will ensure that everyone will have a blanket and a place to sleep? Or should we even care? There are always those around who tell us to "get yours while you can before someone else does." It was maybe this kind of thinking that led to the death of Jdimytai Damour a few years back. He was trampled to death in a Walmart store by frenzied shoppers on Black Friday, the day after Thanksgiving. We are patriotic Americans. We want more things! Take care not to get trampled please. Your life is more precious than any bargain offered at any store.

I pray for enlightened leadership. I look deep into my own heart trying to find a solution to such profound problems. My heart tells me to tend to my own backyard; that what I do there is what the world and all my neighbors need. Sometimes it's a lonely journey. As the old gospel song says, "You have to walk that lonesome valley. You have to walk it by yourself. Ain't nobody else gonna walk it for you. You have to walk it by yourself." Can we at least hold hands as we continue on? Rather than despair, I rise in the morning, put

Blessed are my siblings, for they bring joy.

on my clothes, comb my hair, brush my teeth, and bow to the eastern sun with gratitude for another day.

Mixed with other duties, I find time to till my garden, knowing that the sun, rain, and Mother Earth will work their magic on the precious seeds I hold in my hand. I find joy holding my own children and now grandchildren, some who live too far away, telling them I love them, giving them hugs, telling them stories, and showing them where to look for bees, snakes (yes, even snakes), ladybugs, birds, and butterflies that are as sacred as themselves. I give joyful thanks for the wholesome soup and fresh-made meals that my wife prepares to keep our bodies strong and heal our spirits. I am eternally grateful that I have a blanket and a warm place to sleep.

Please tell me, is there something else in life that I should be doing?

"Rather than despair, I rise in the morning, put on my clothes, comb my hair, brush my teeth, and bow to the eastern sun with gratitude for another day."

—Larry Haun

CREDITS

All photos/drawings courtesy Larry Haun except where noted